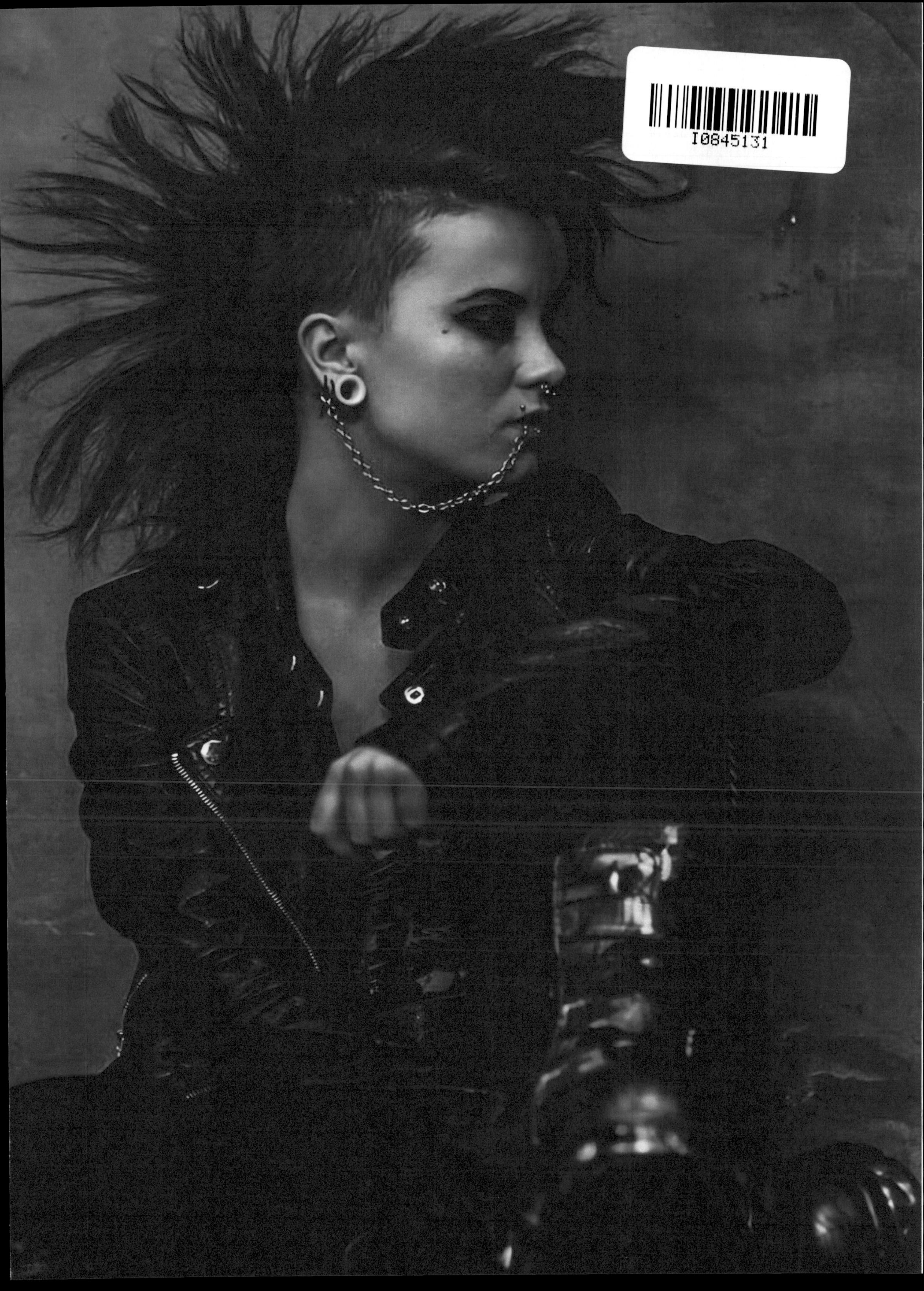

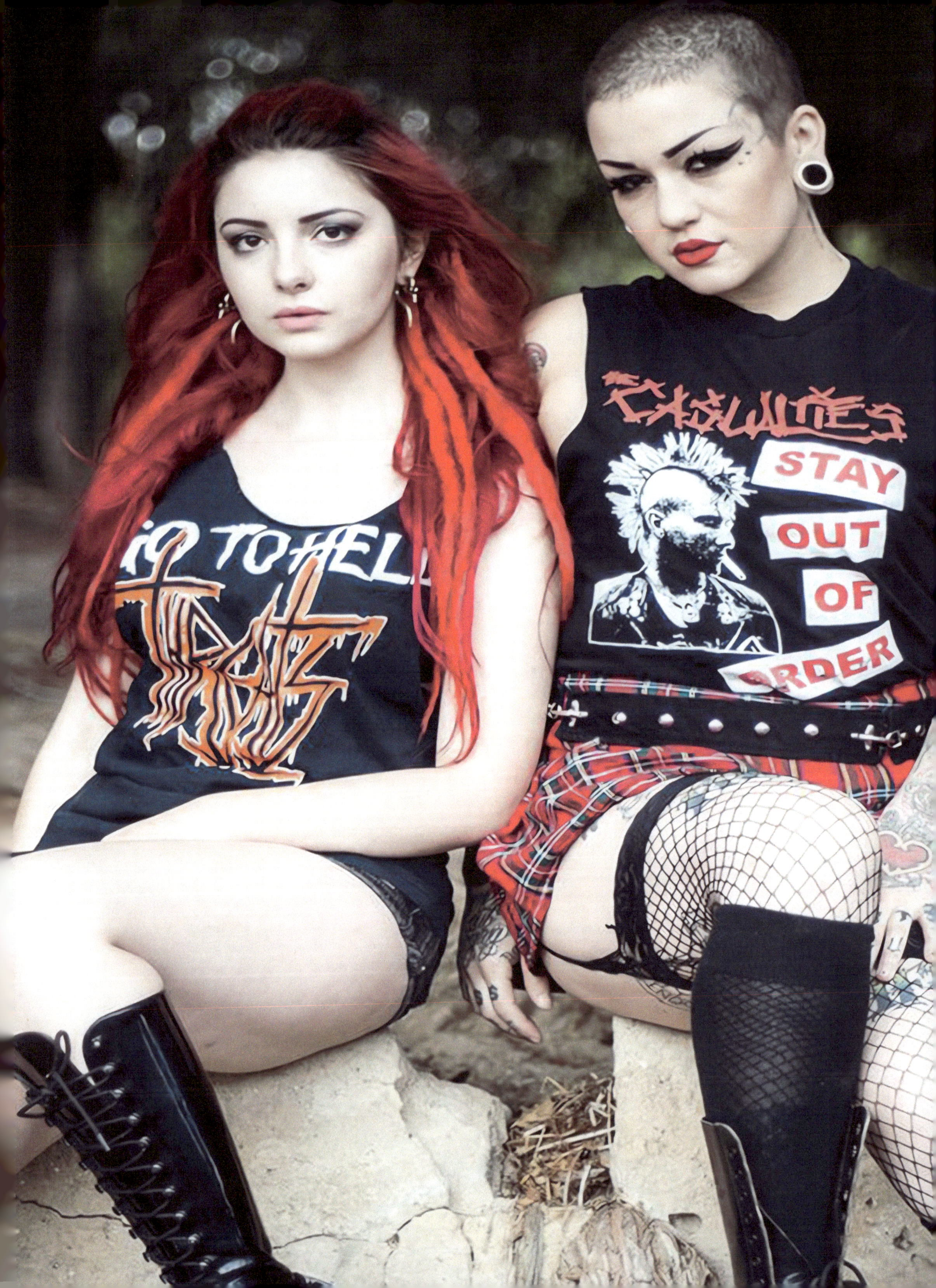
GO TO HELL
THE CASUALTIES
STAY
OUT
OF
ORDER

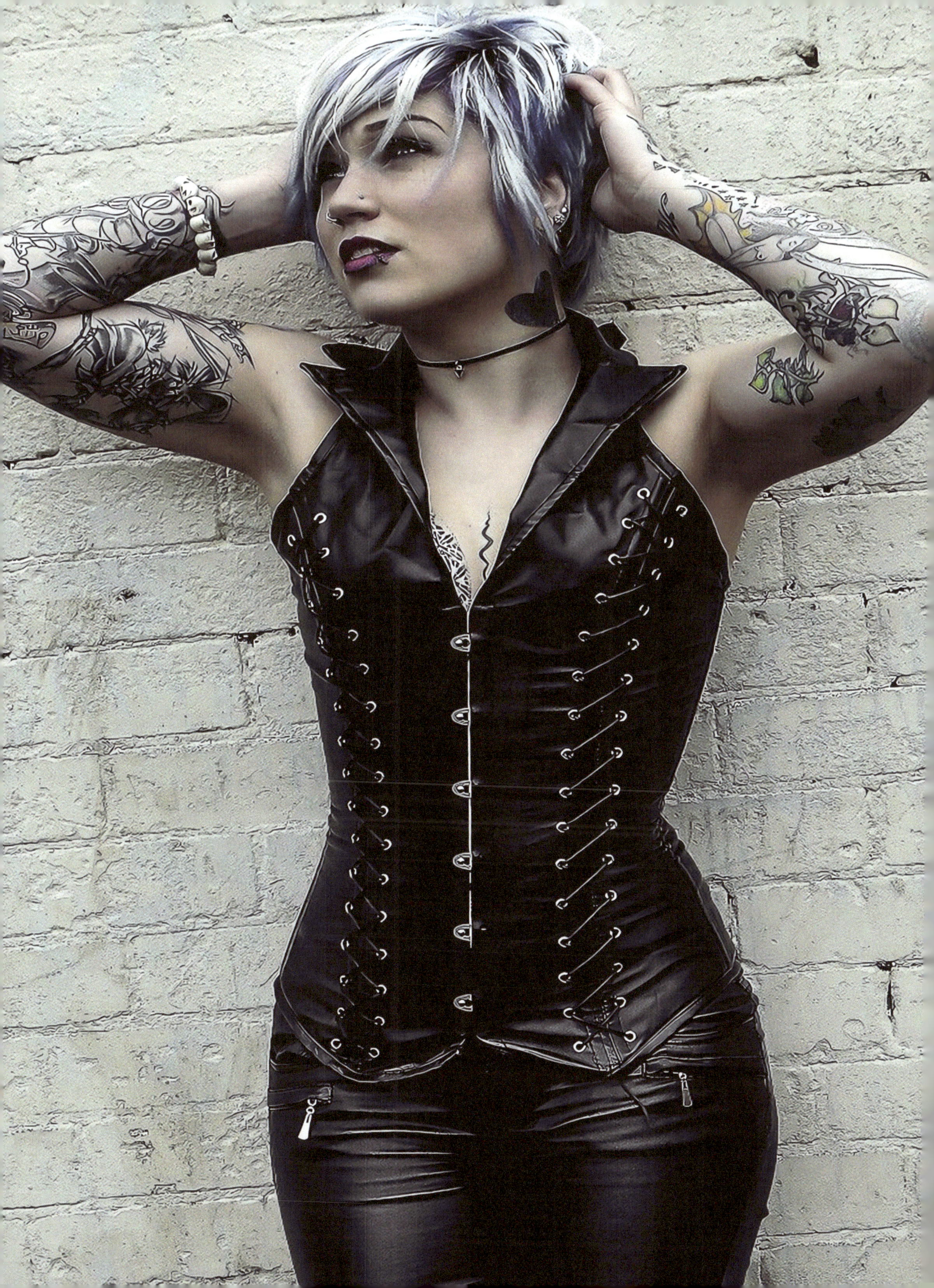

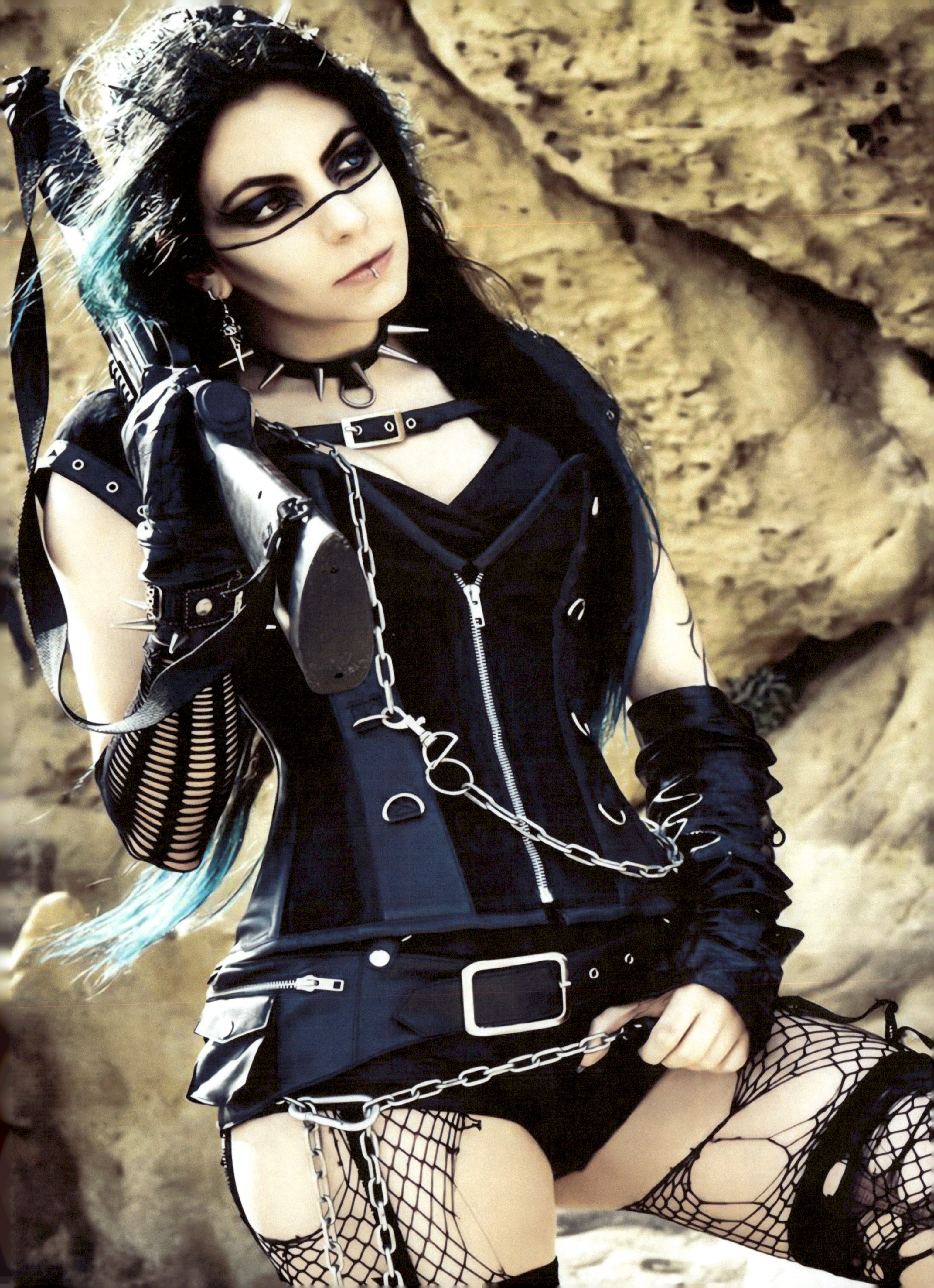

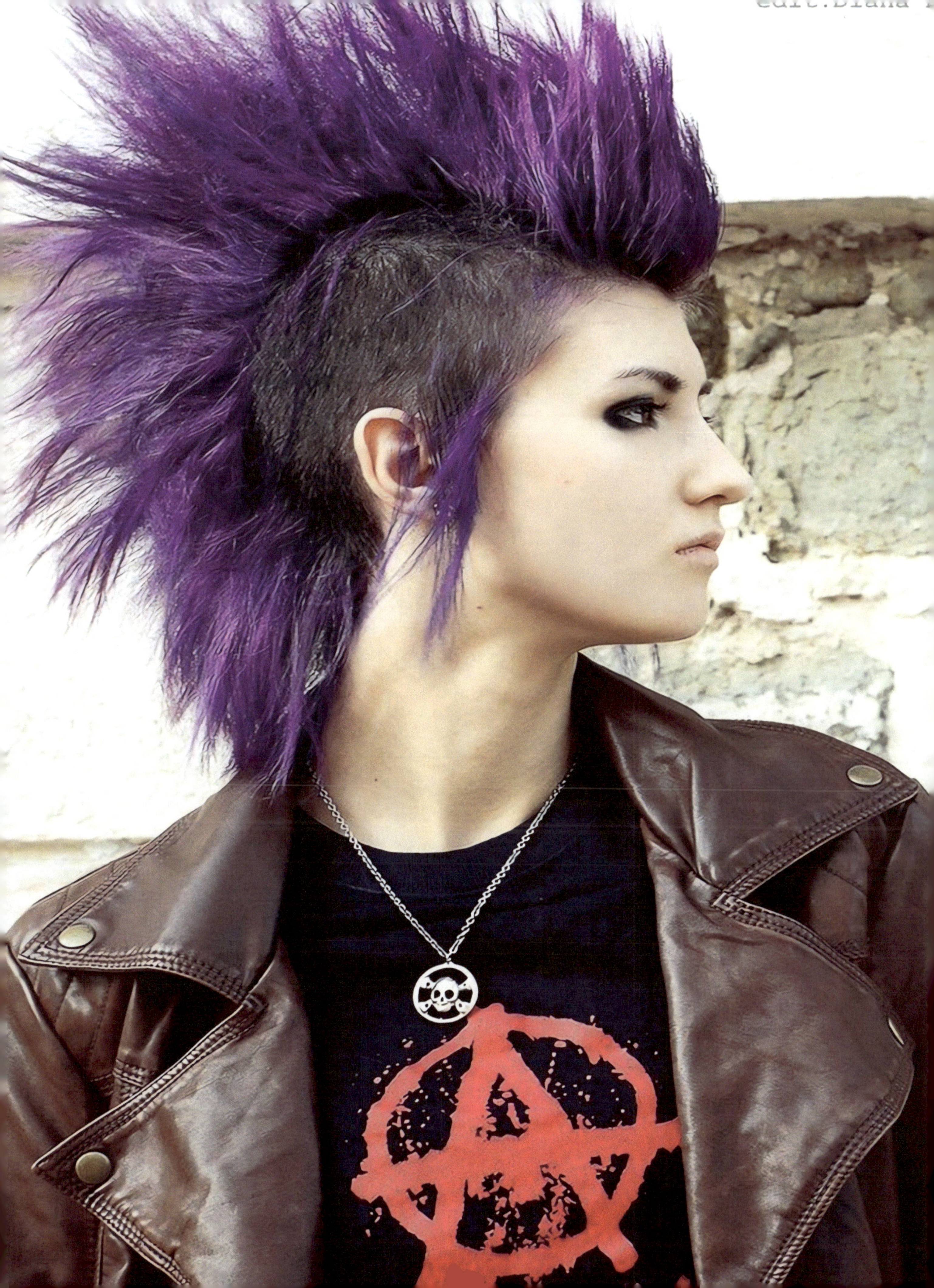
edit.Diana

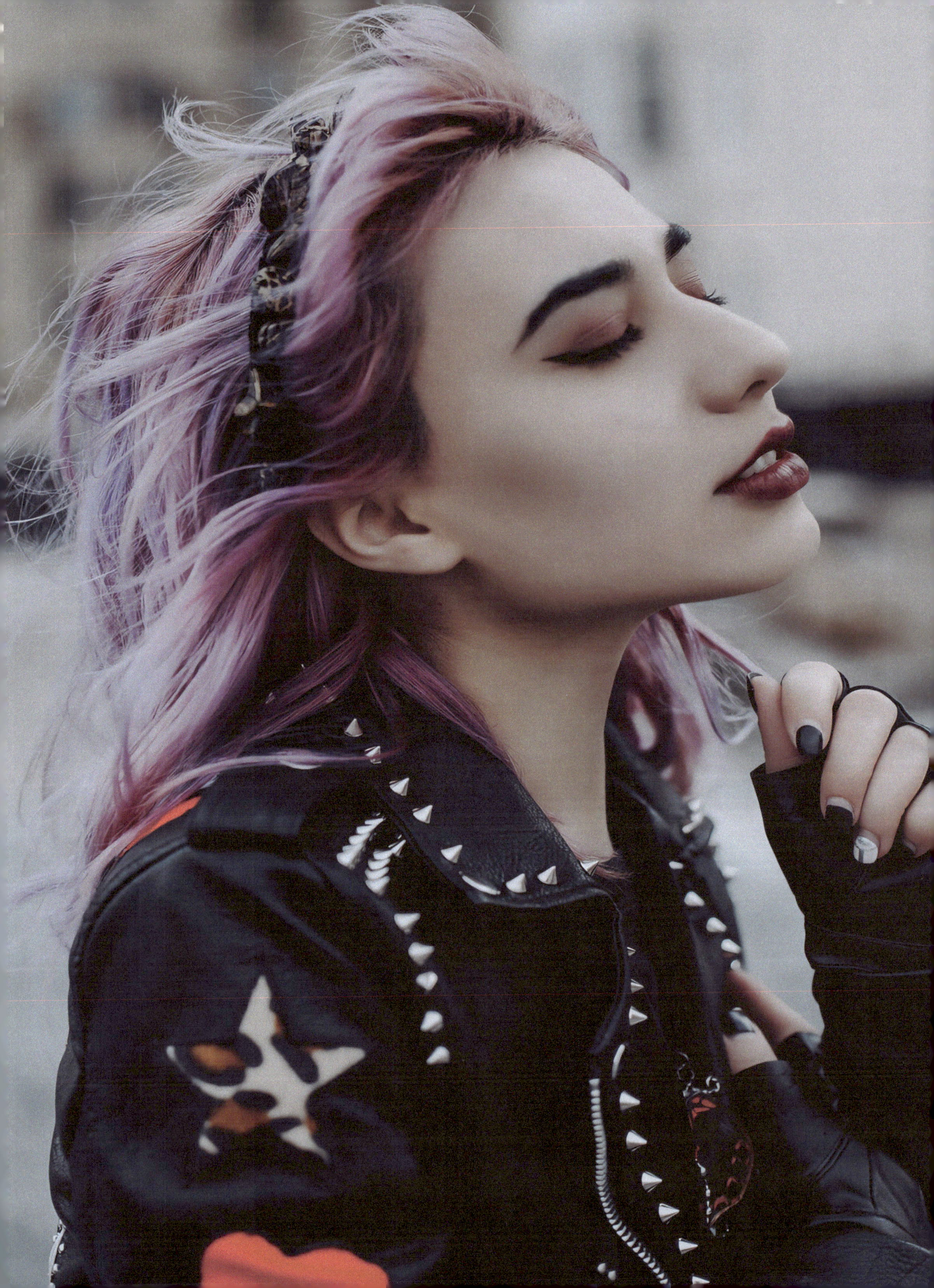

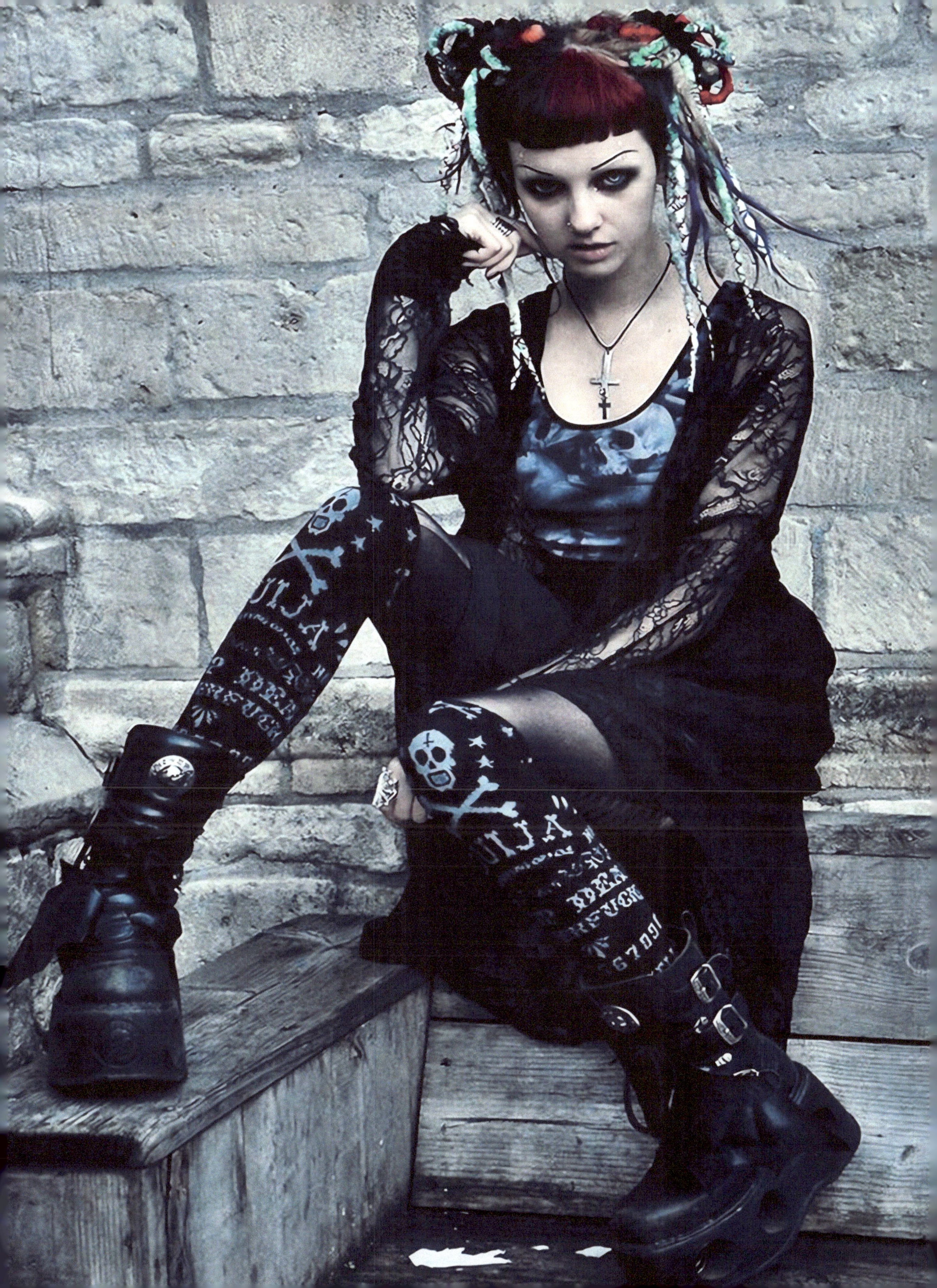

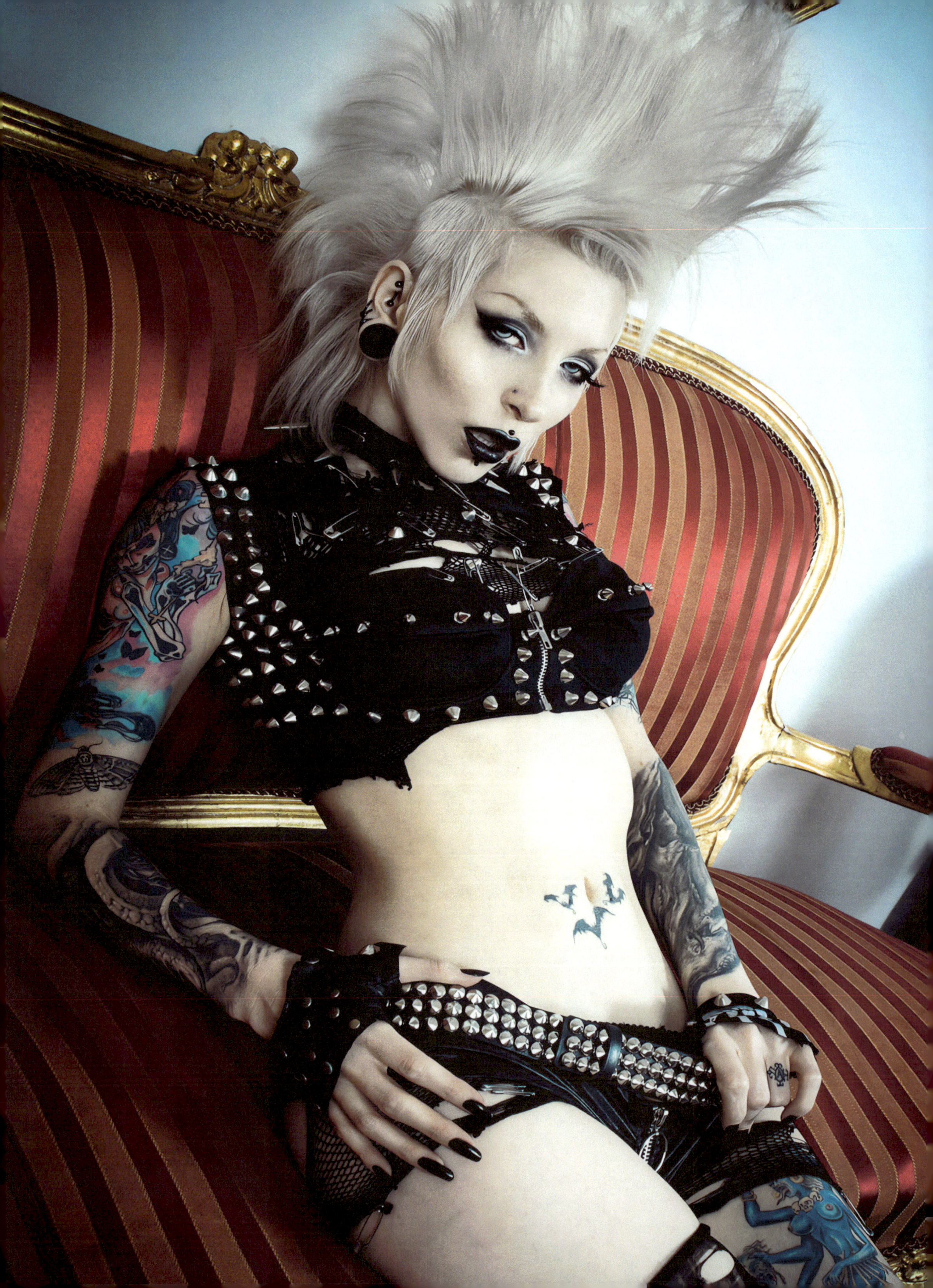

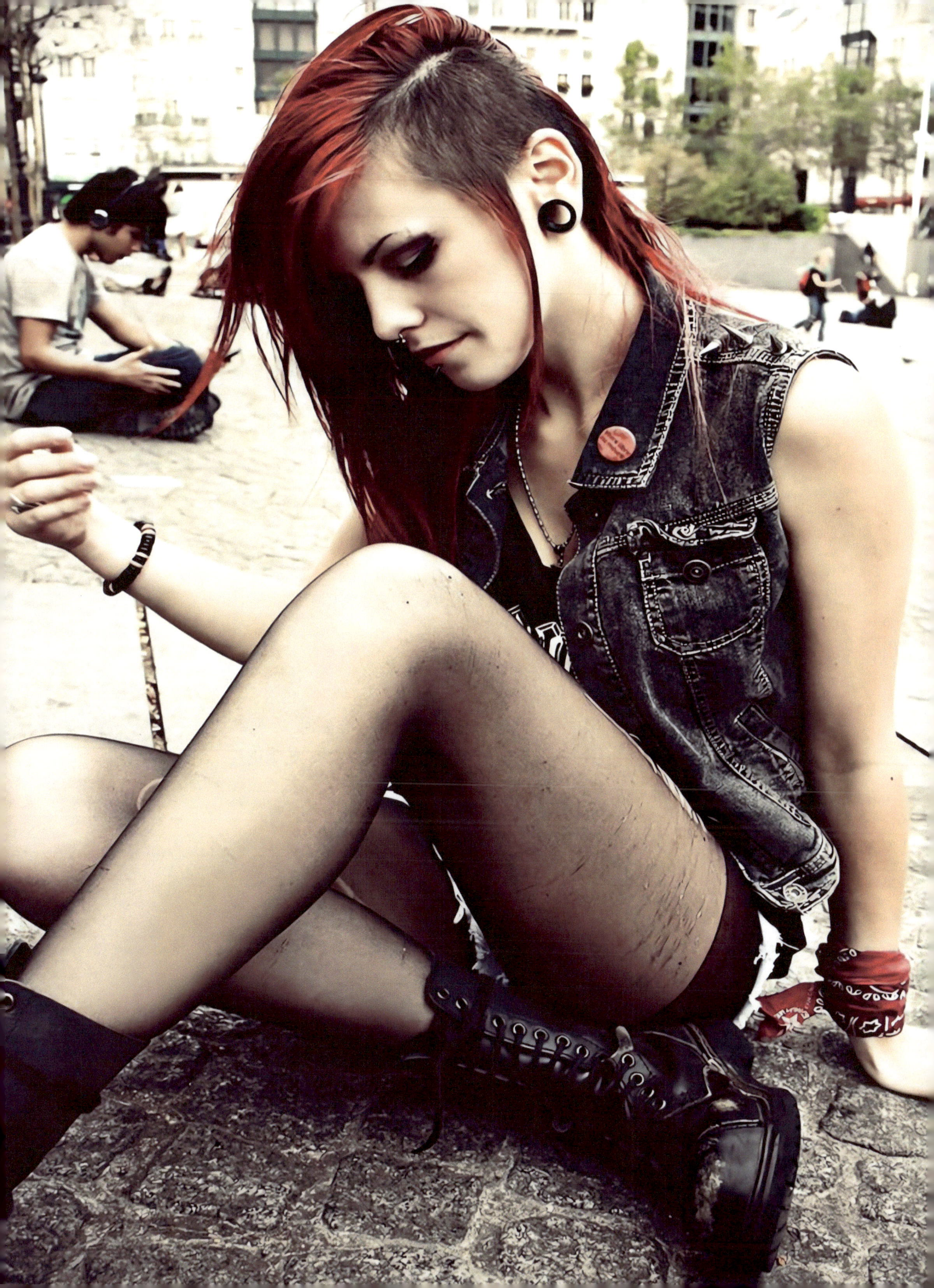

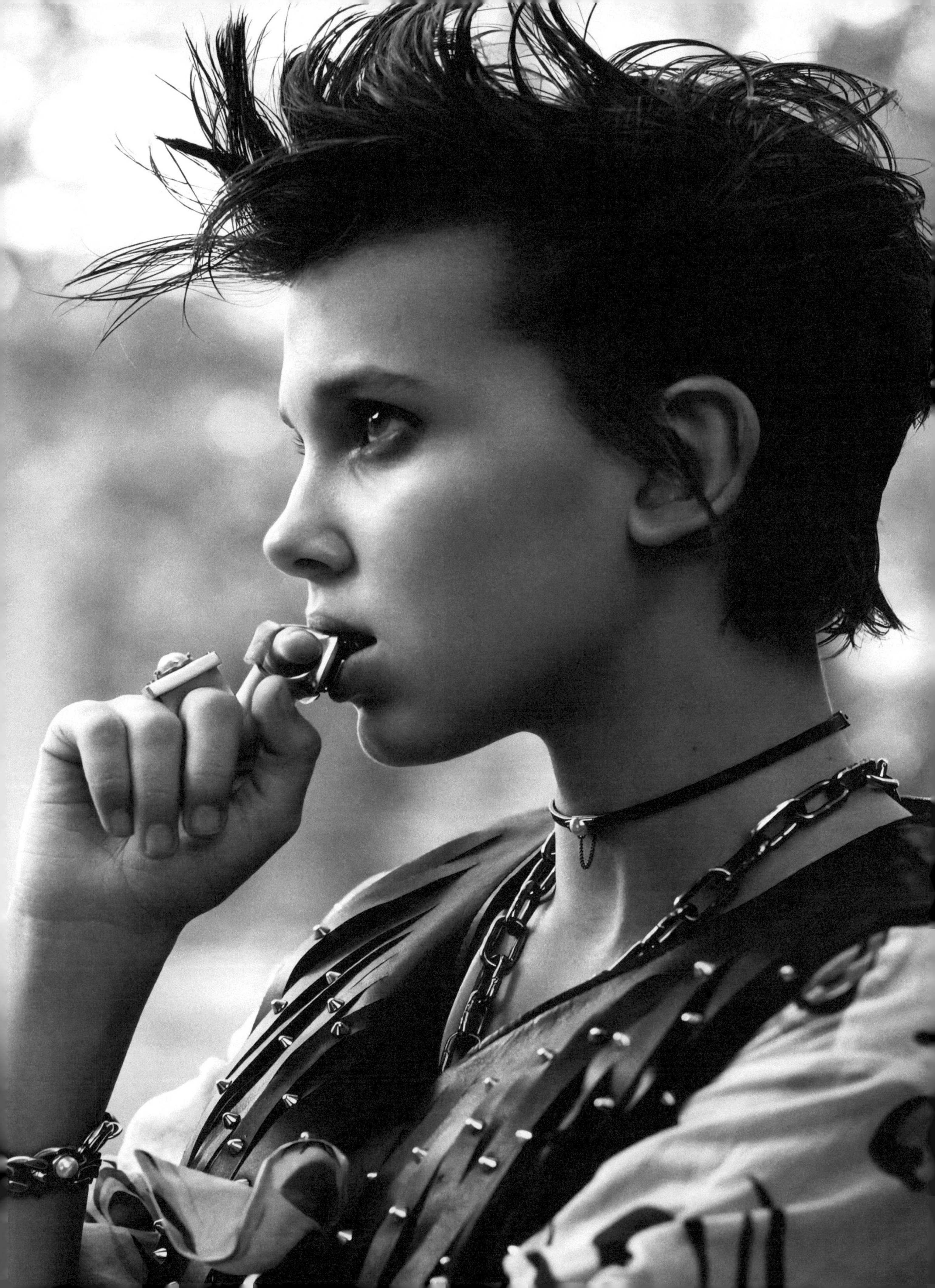

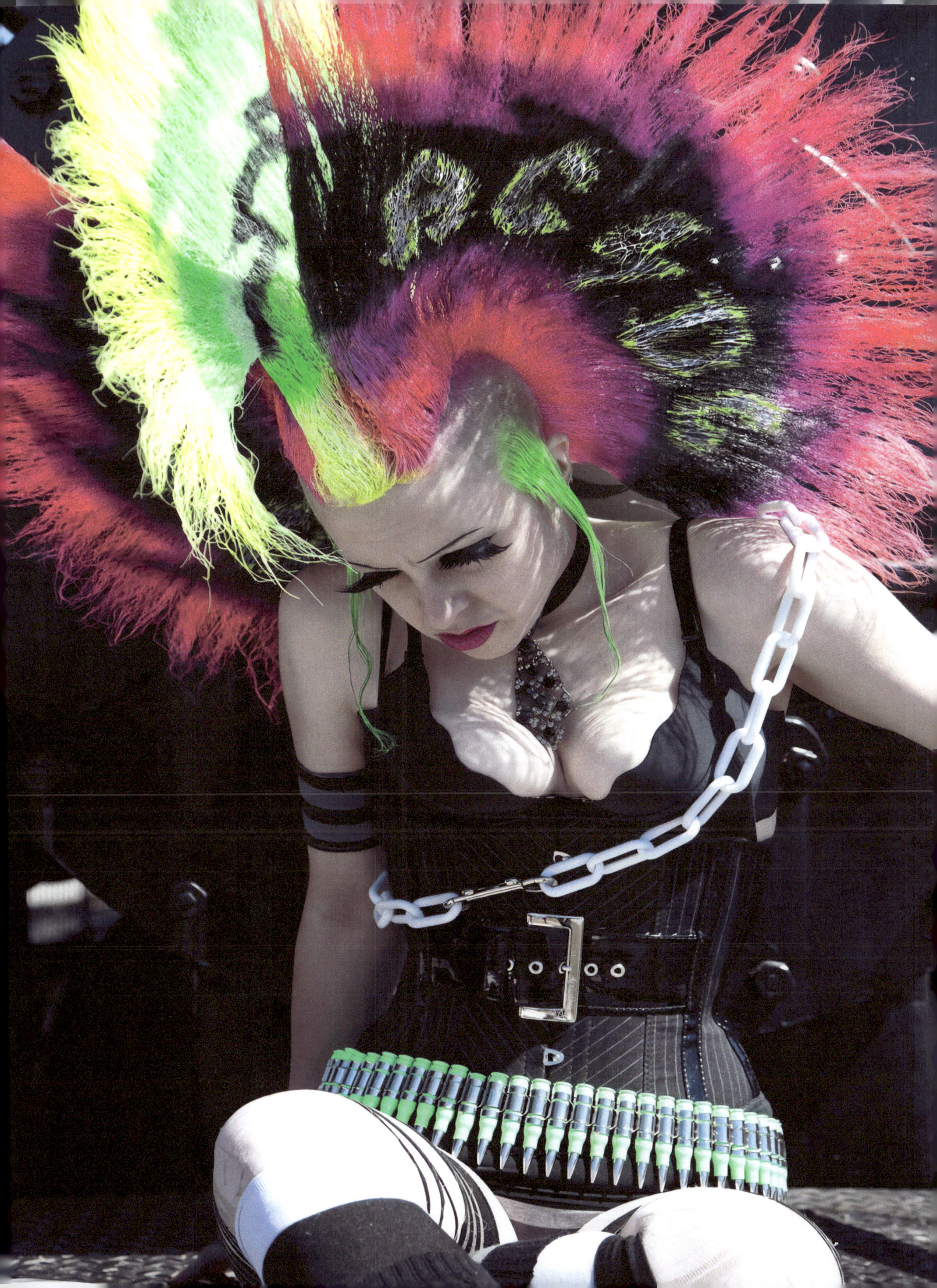

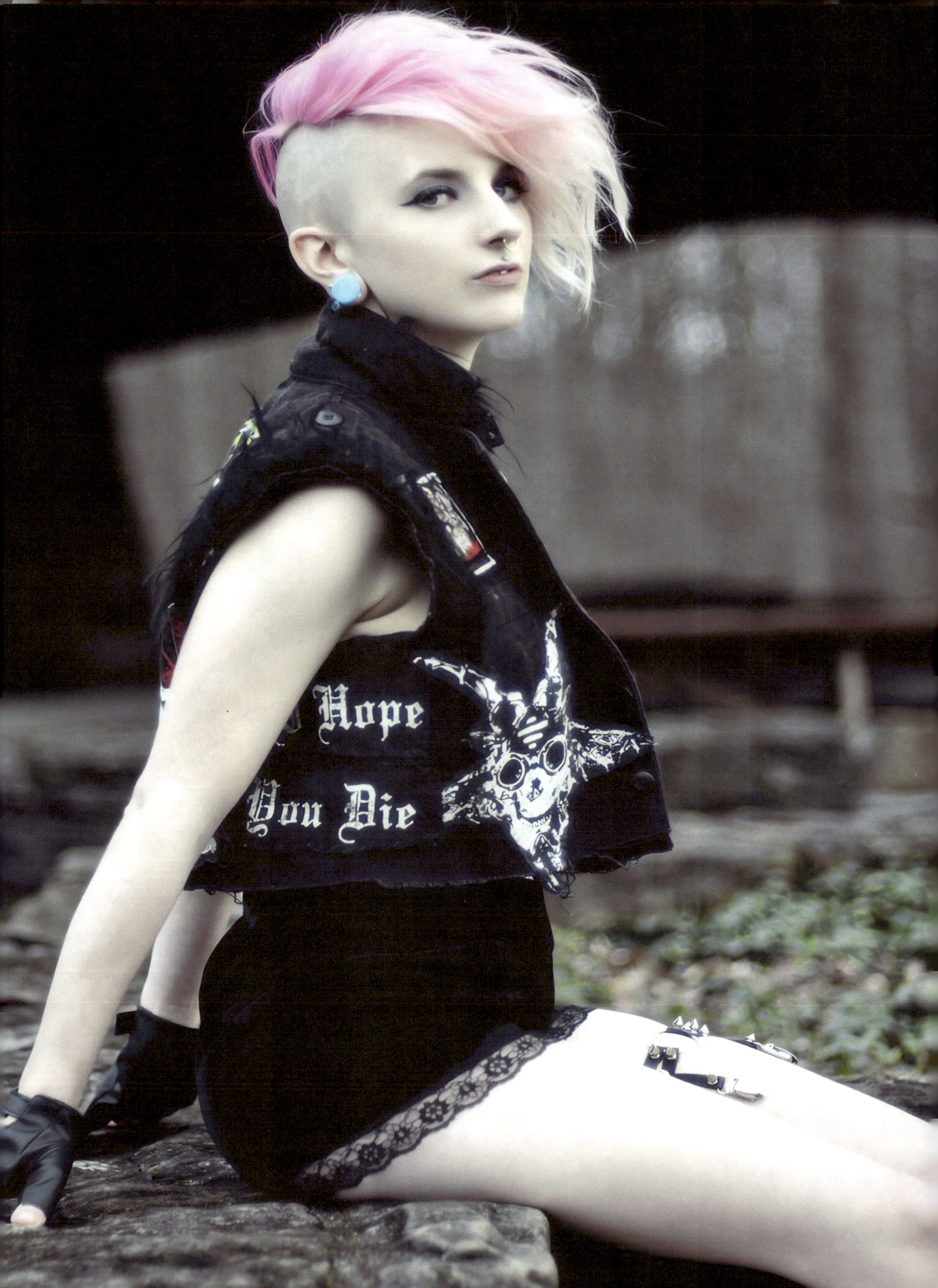
Hope
You Die

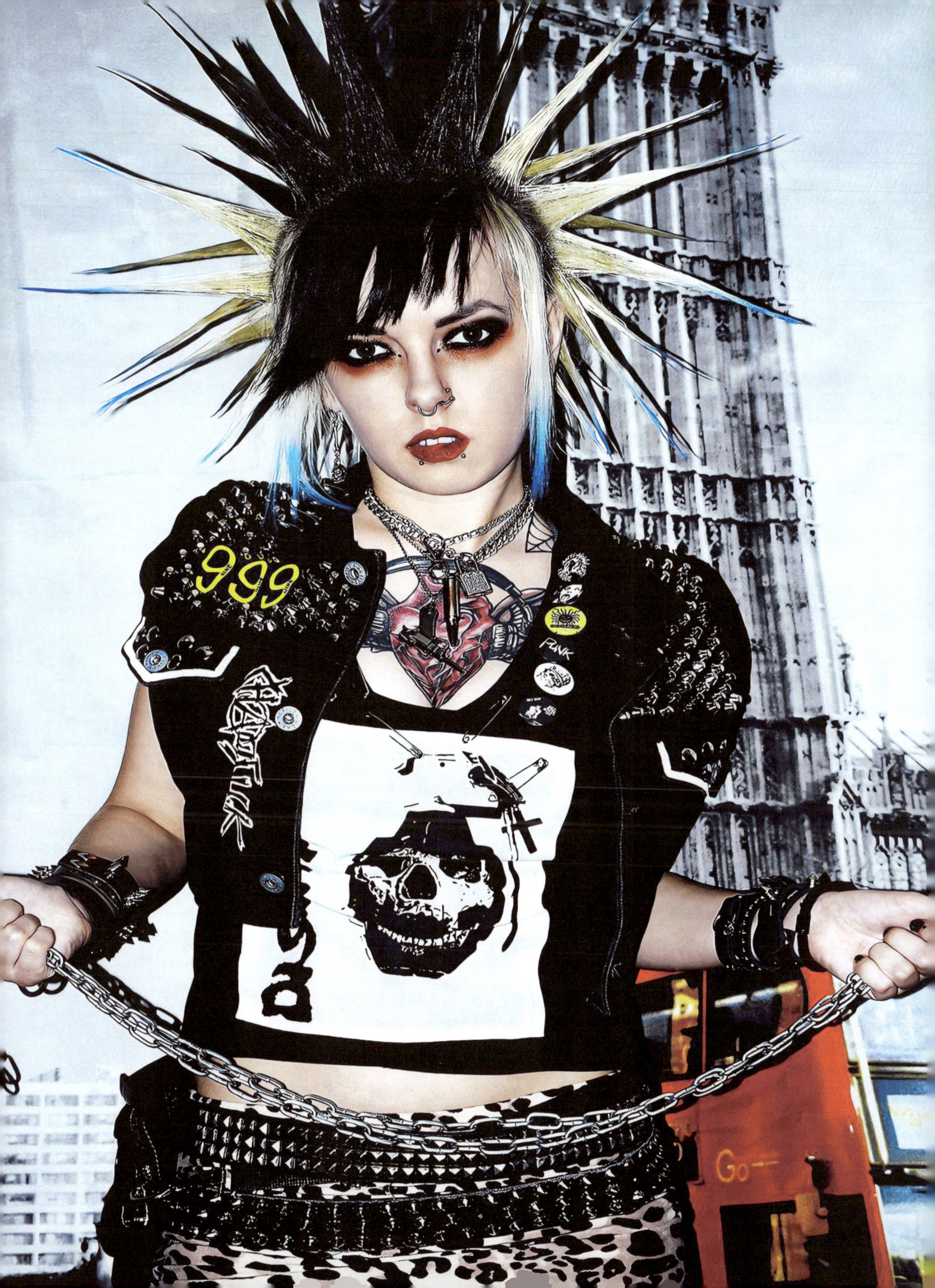
999
PUNK
Go

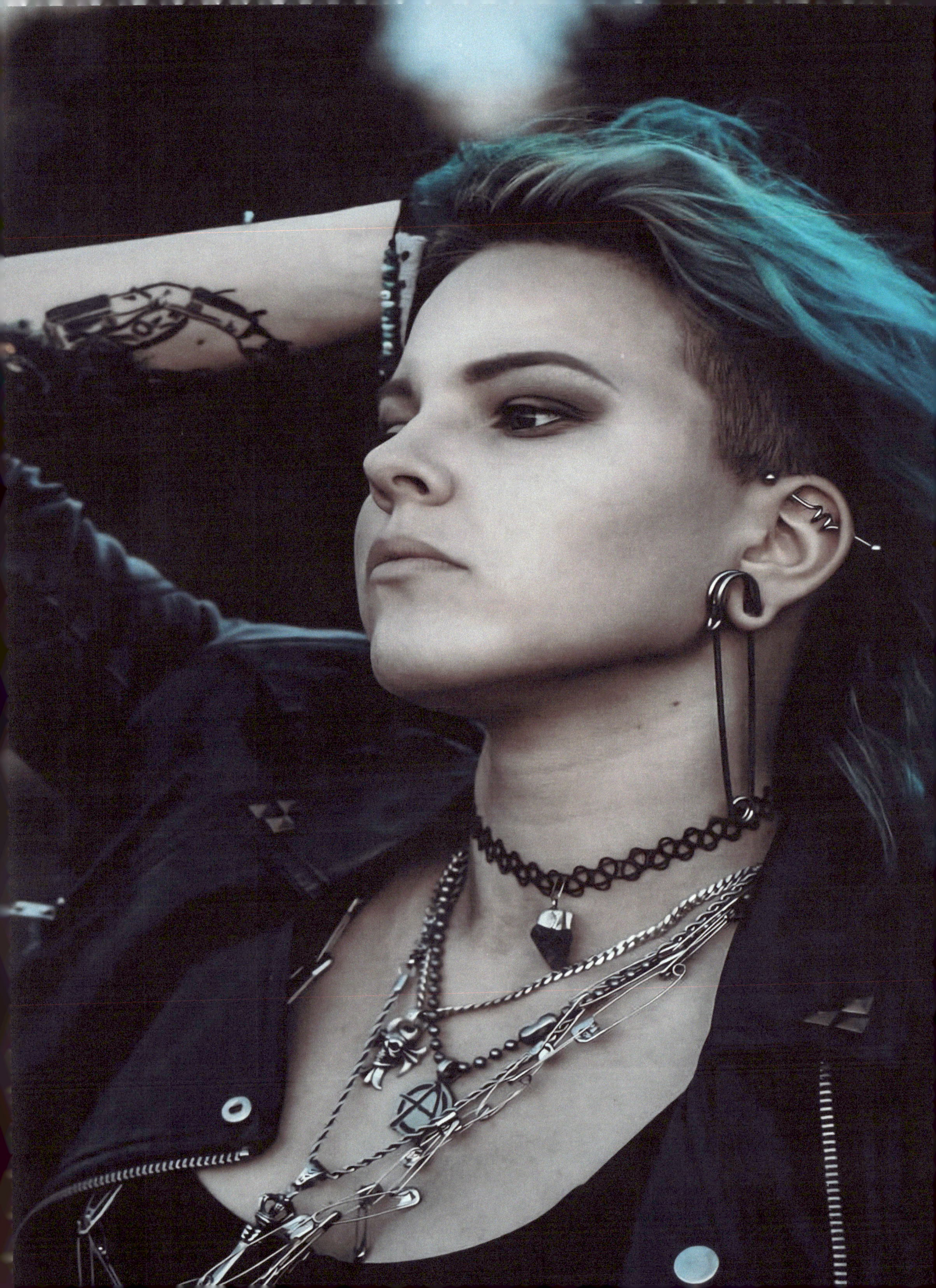

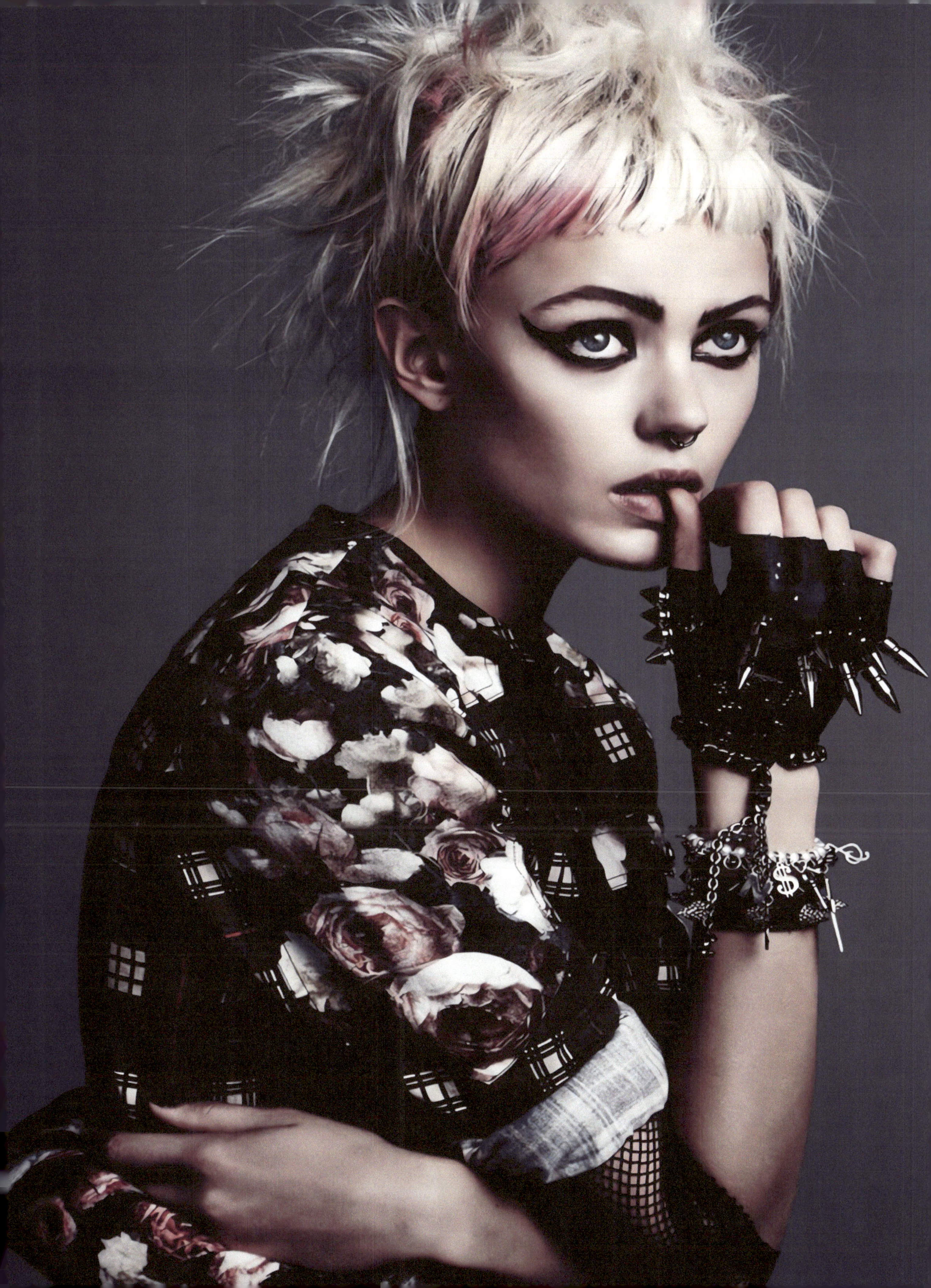

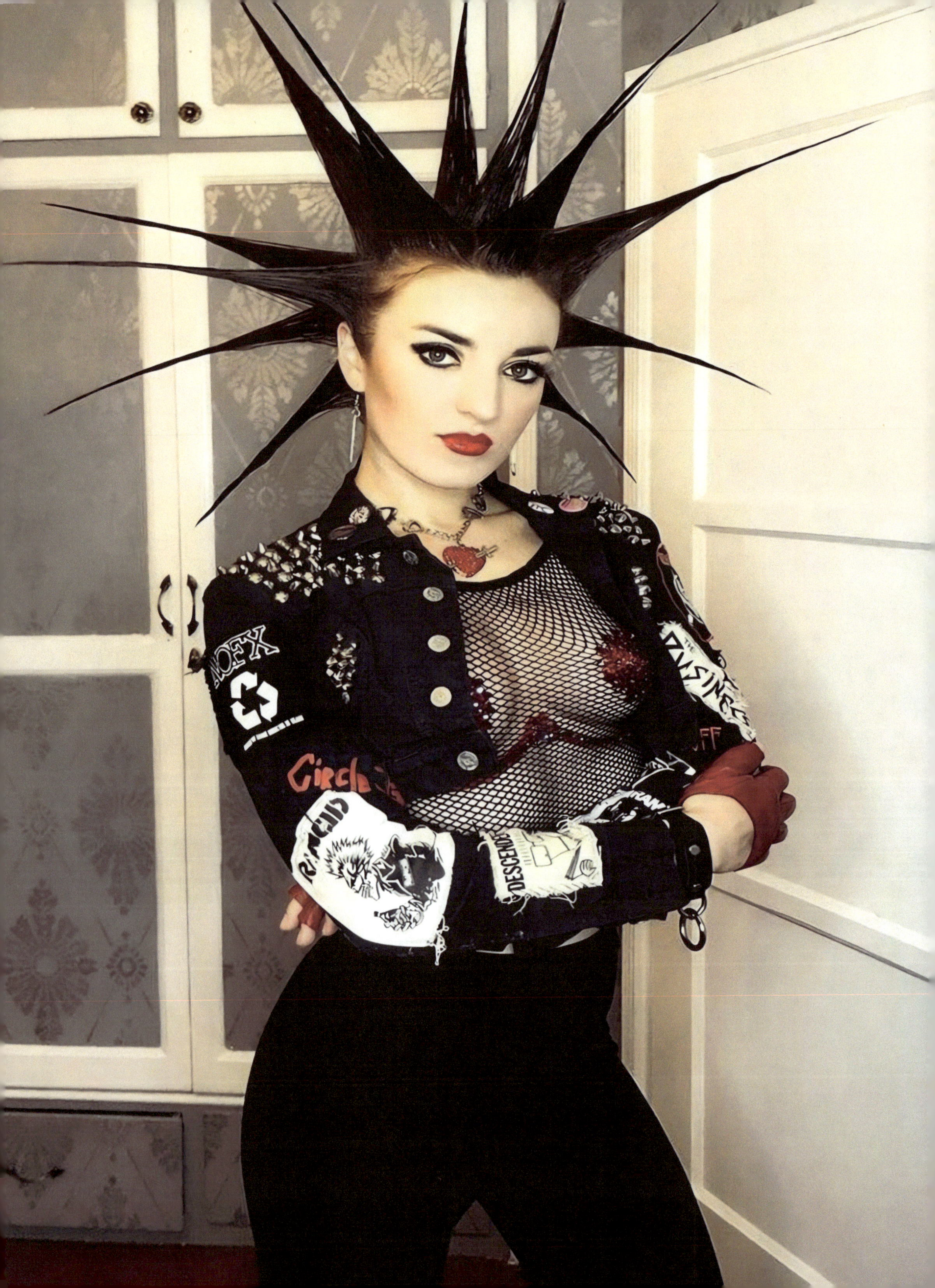

NOFX
Circle
RANCID
DESCENDE
THE BUSINESS

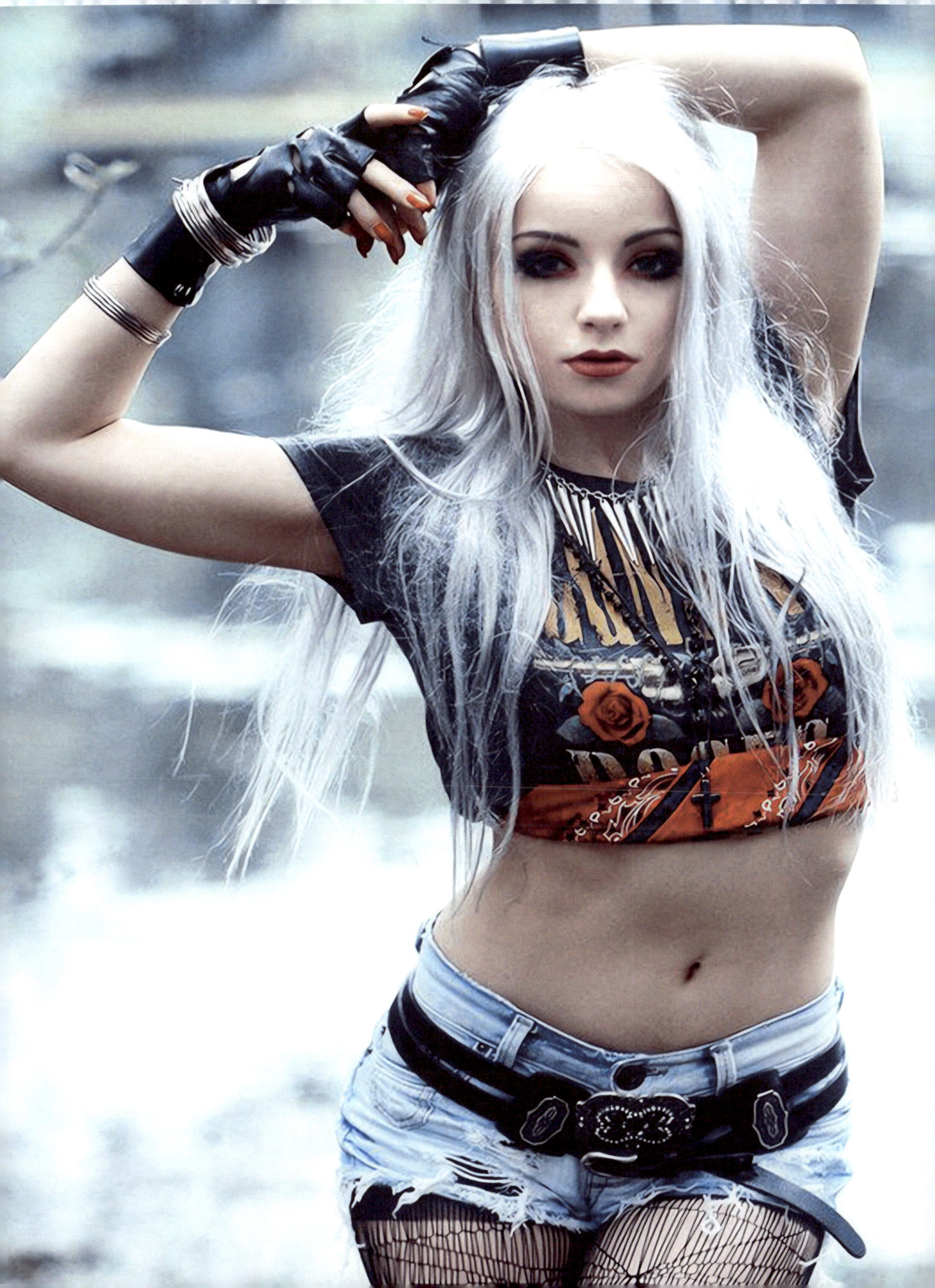

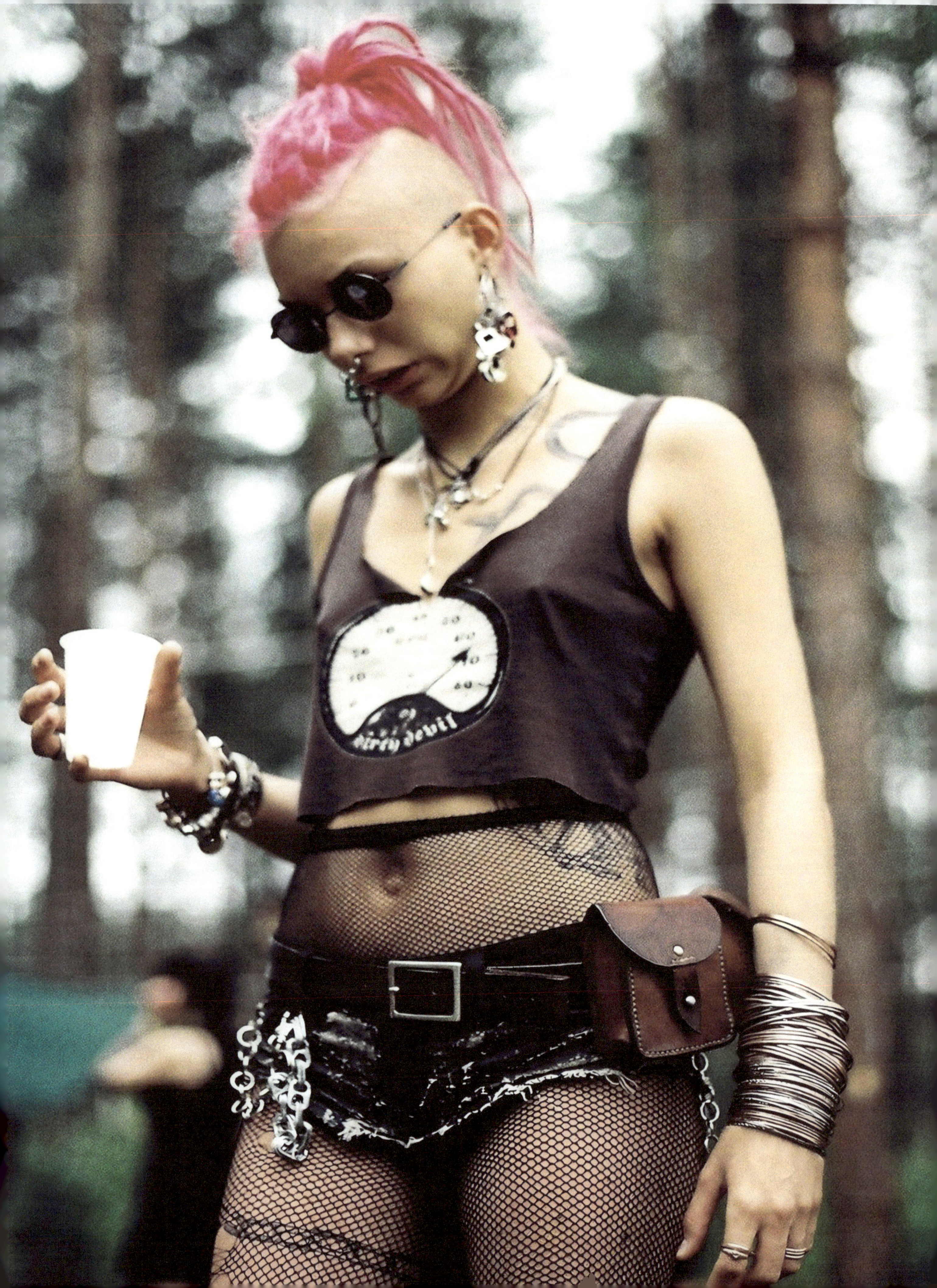

dirty devil

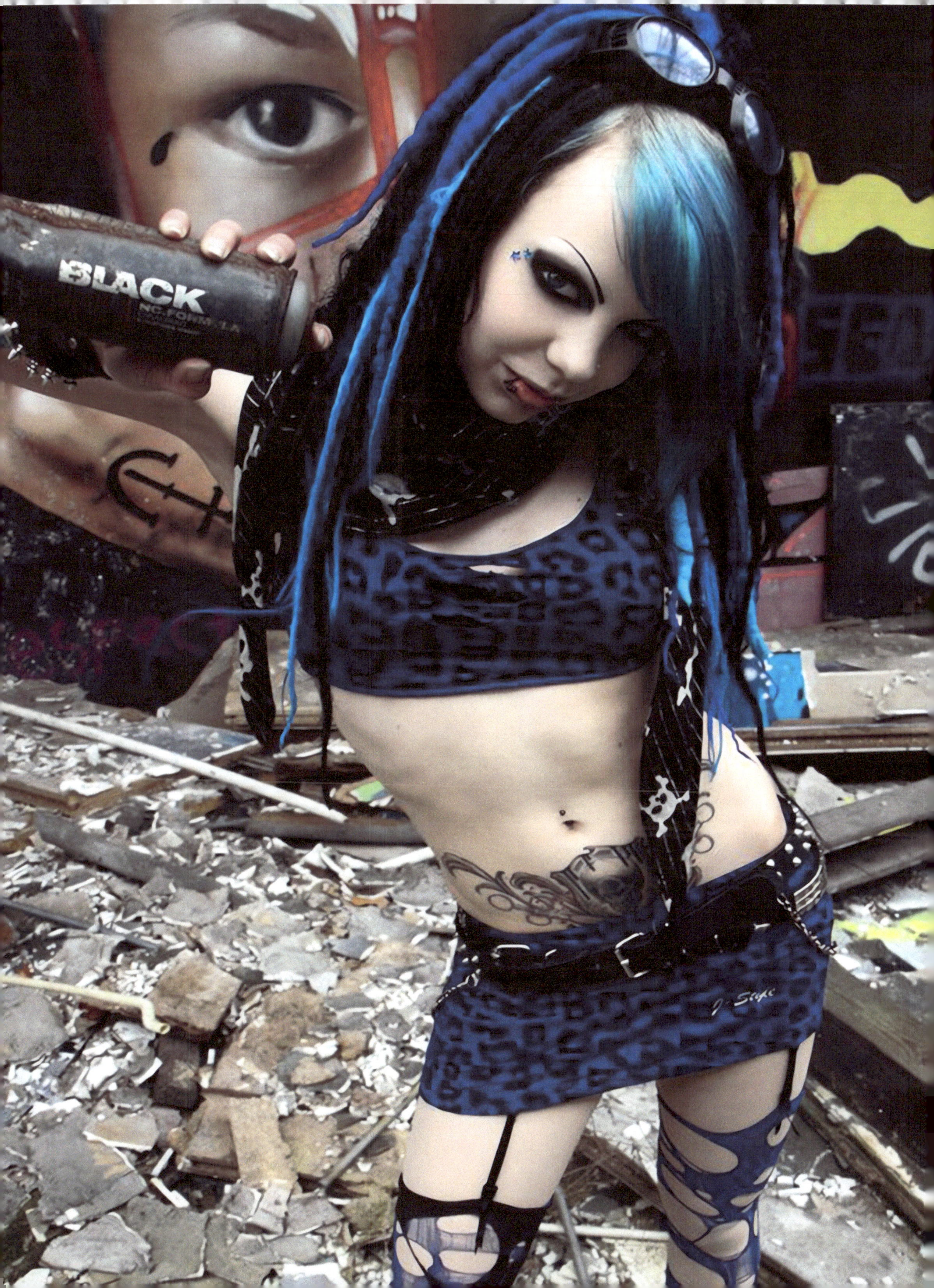

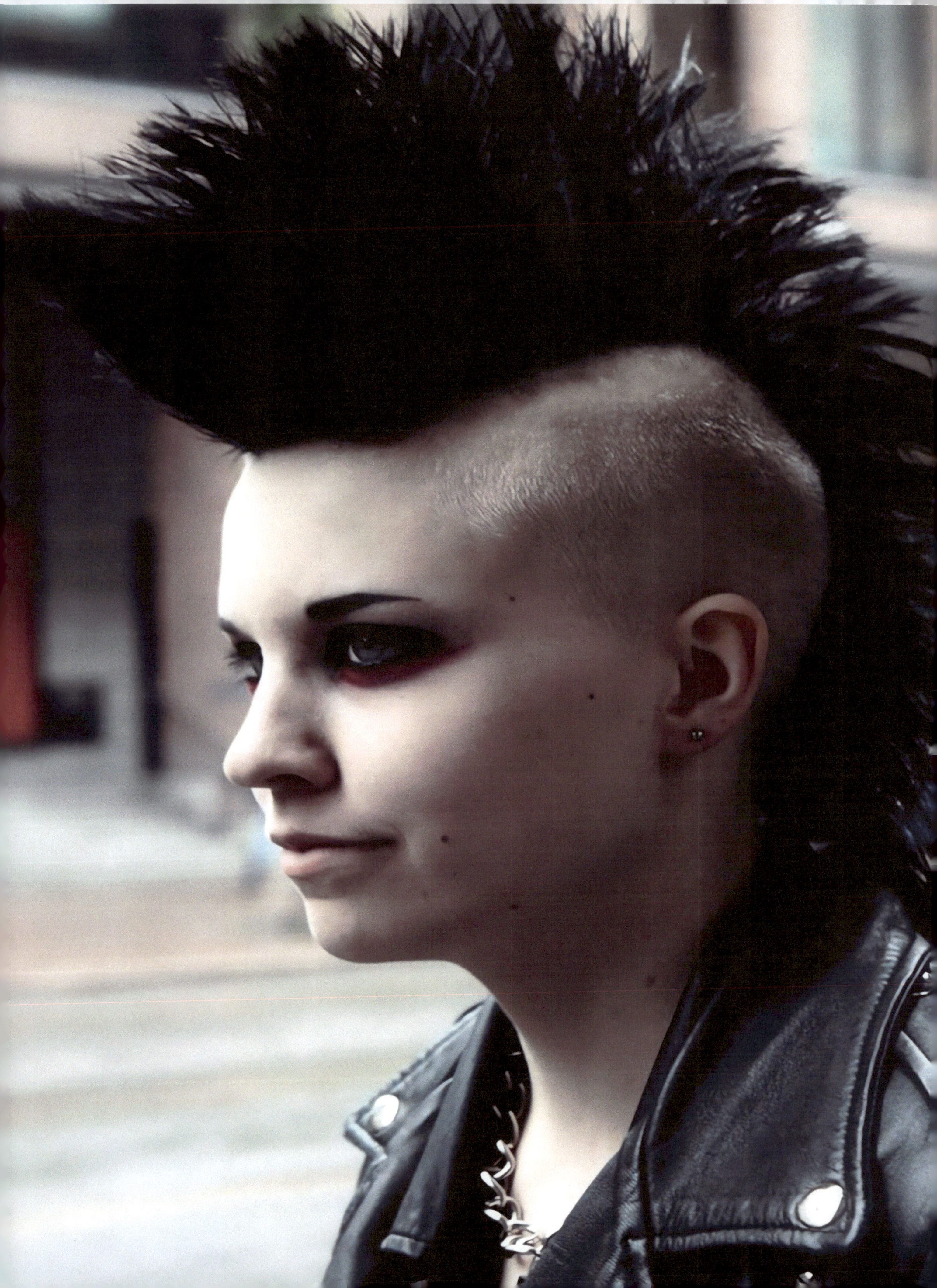

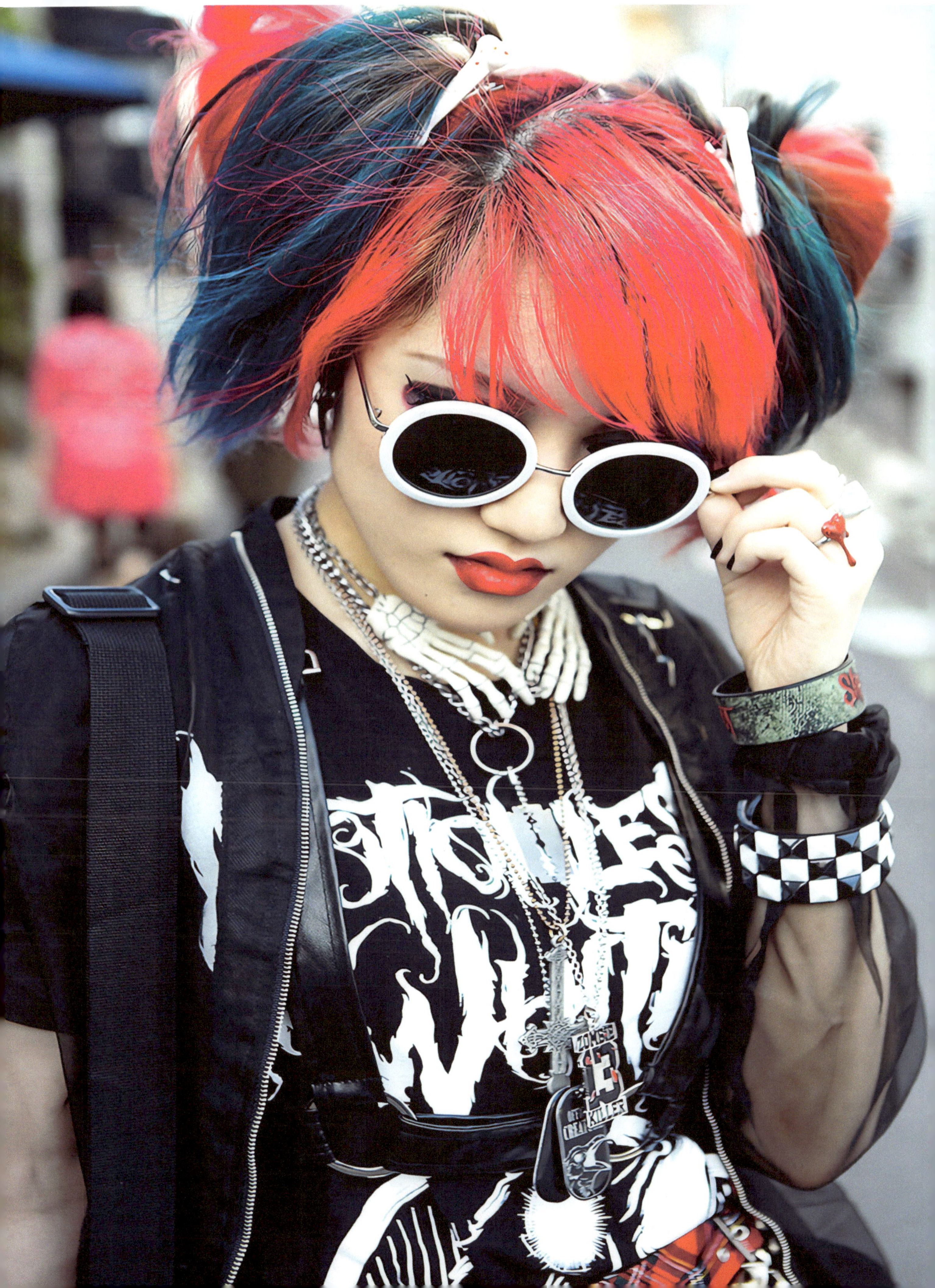

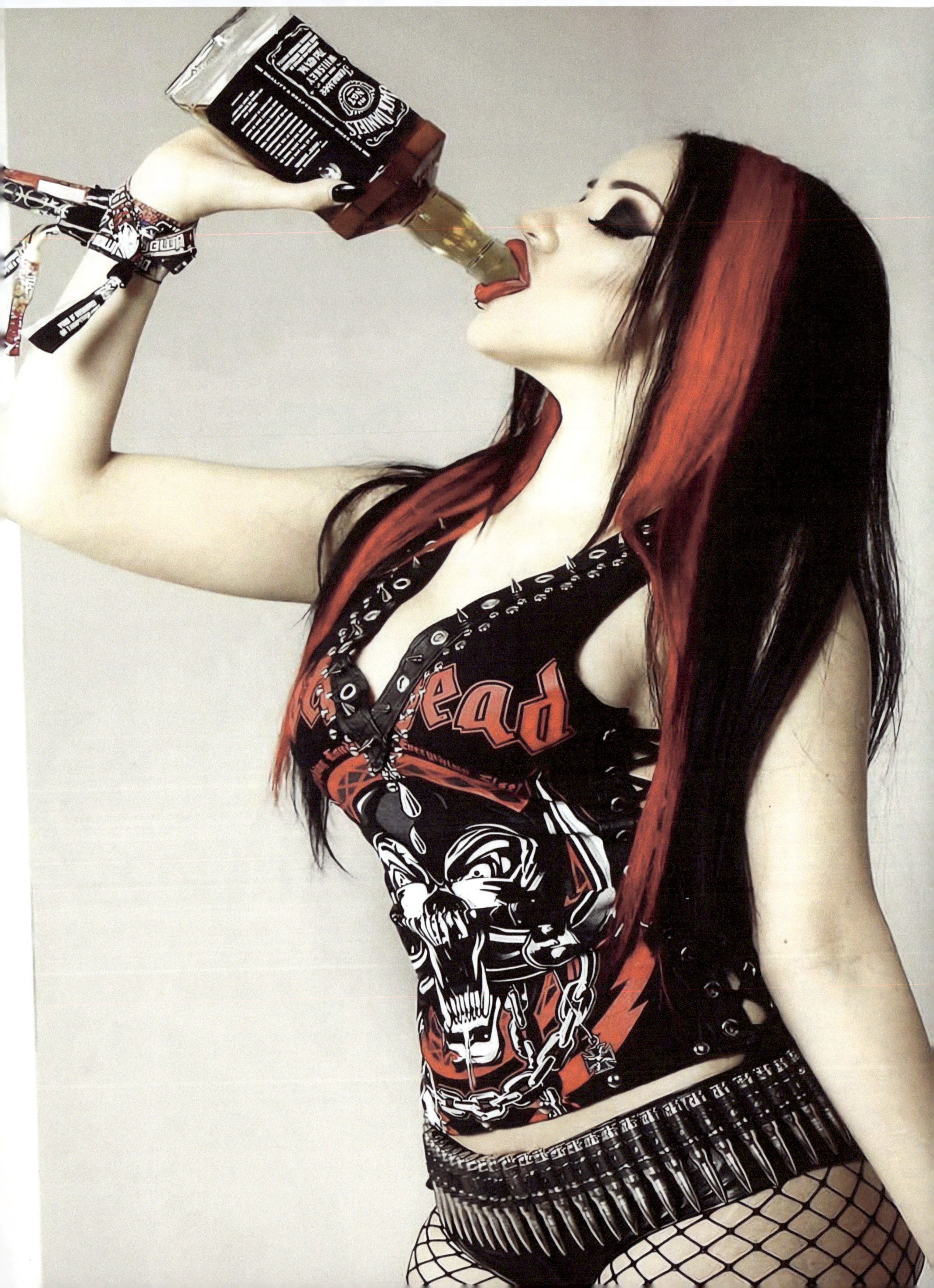

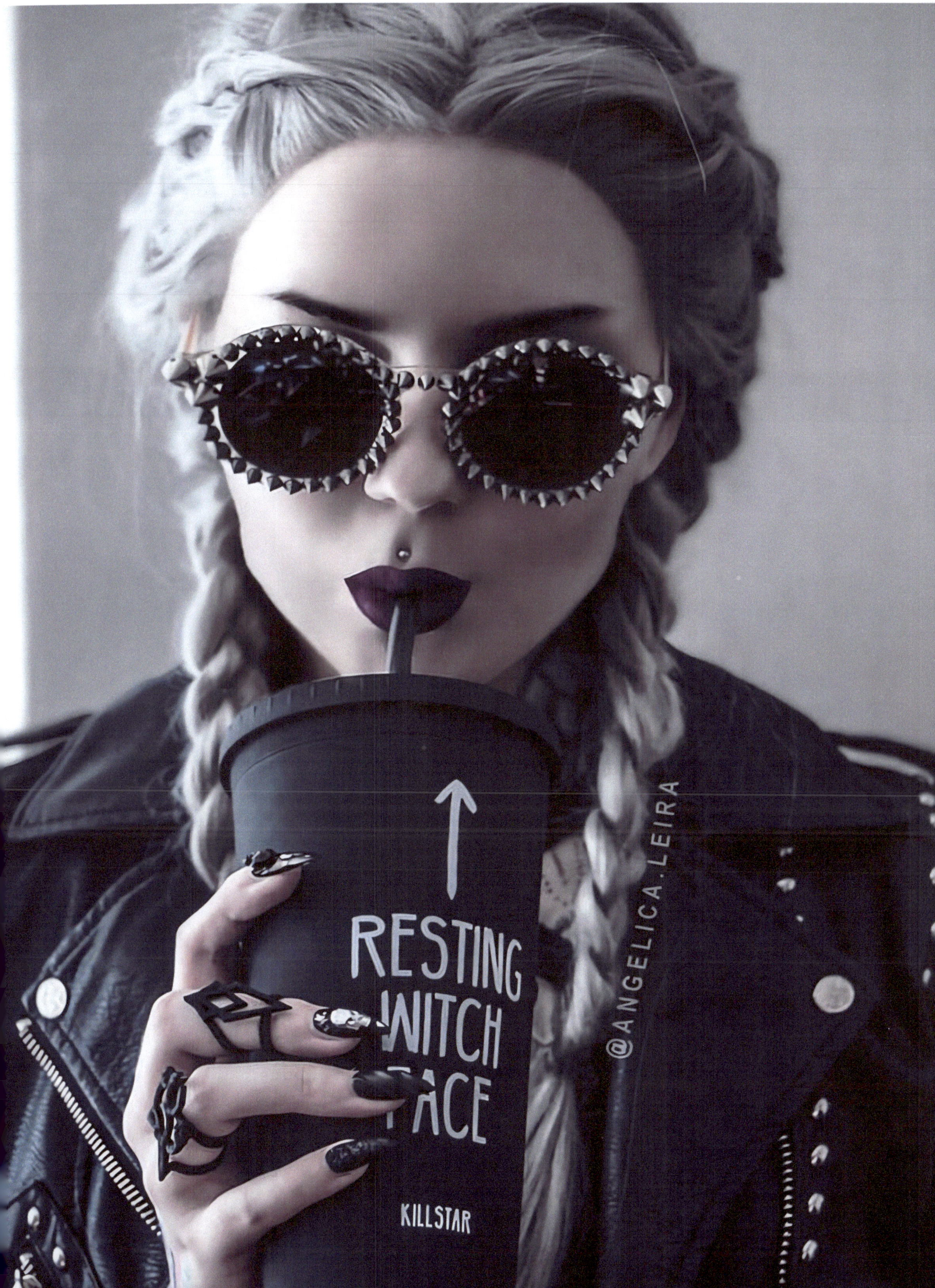

↑
RESTING
WITCH
FACE
KILLSTAR
@ANGELICA.LEIRA

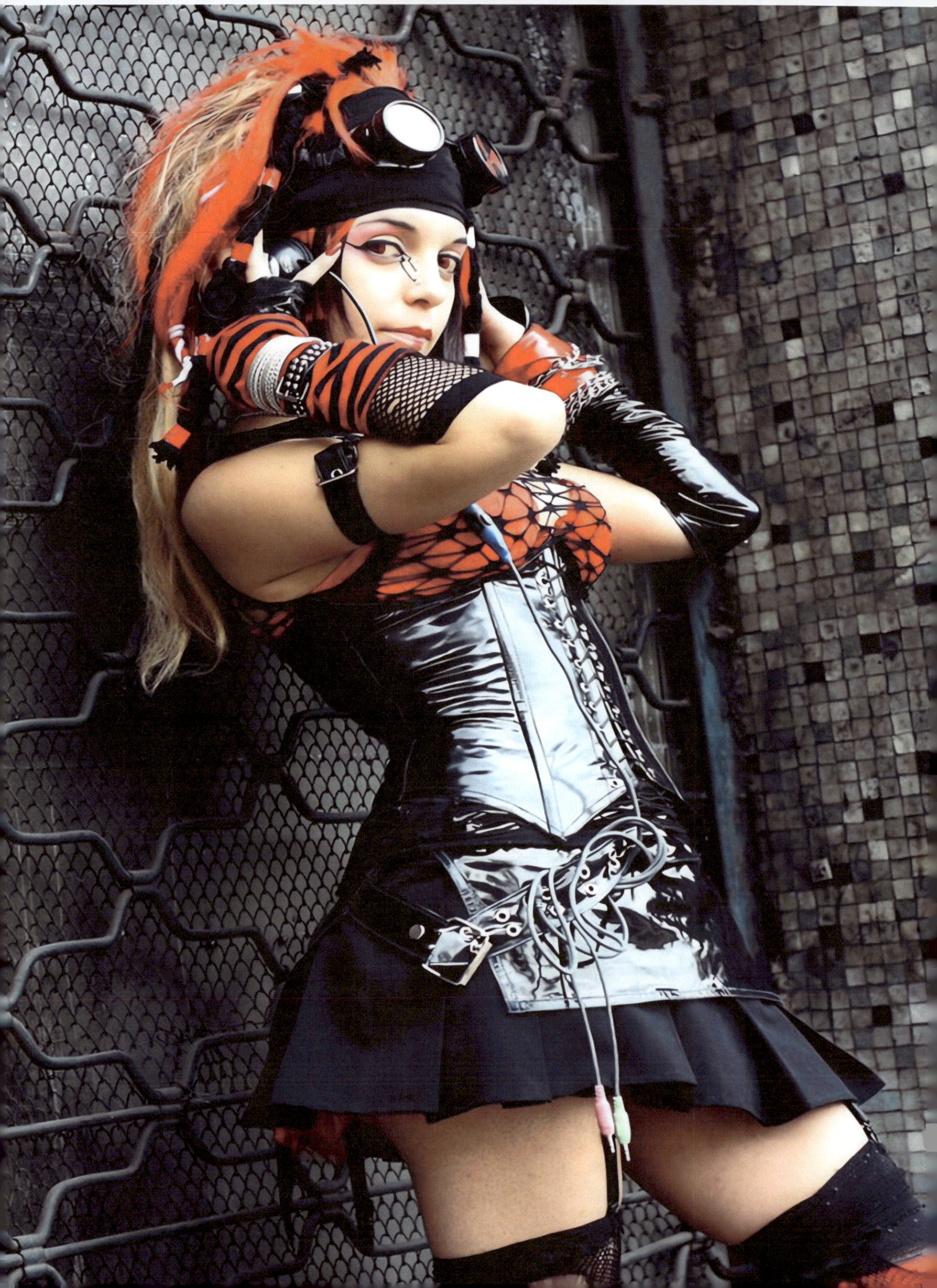

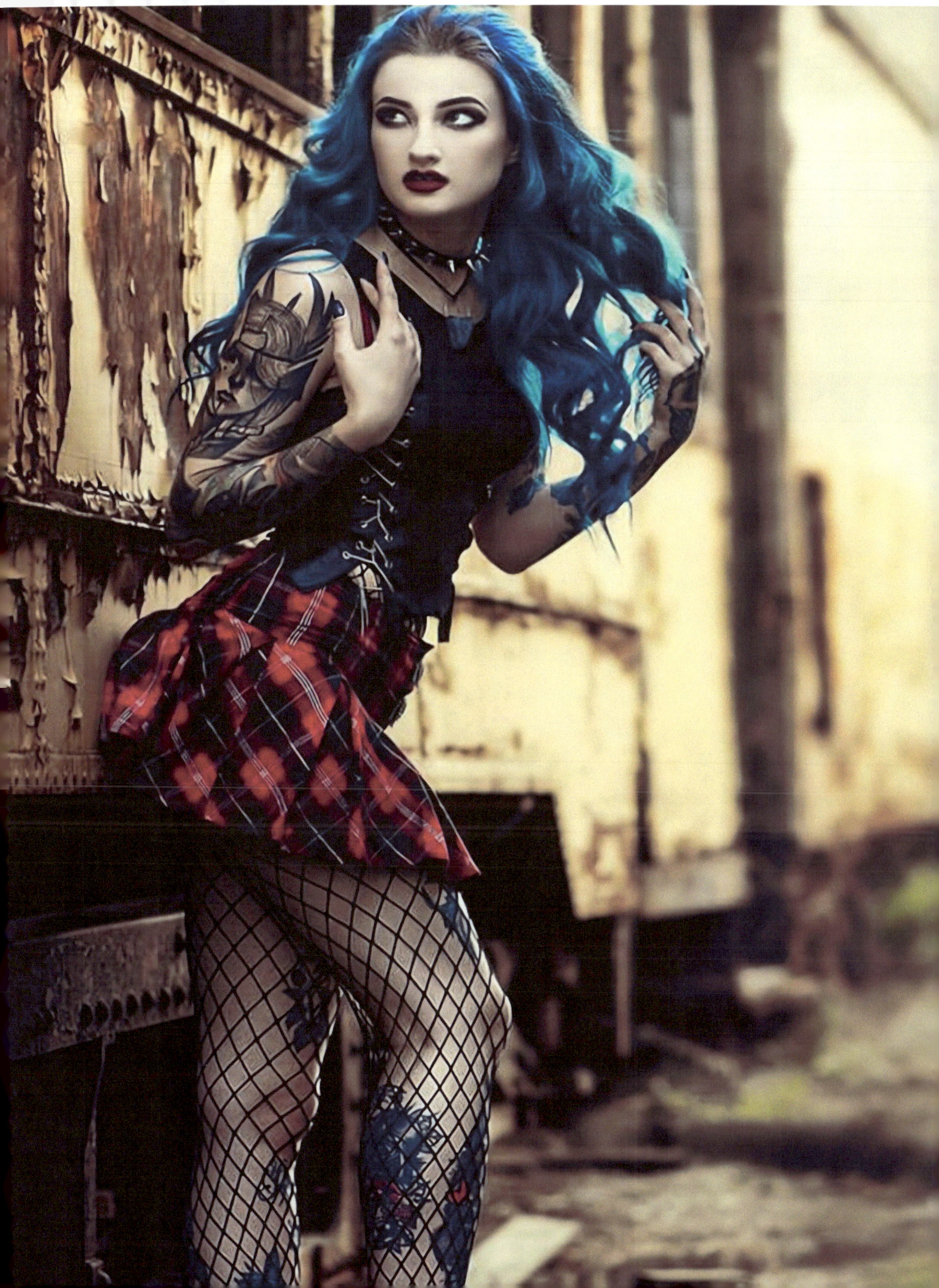

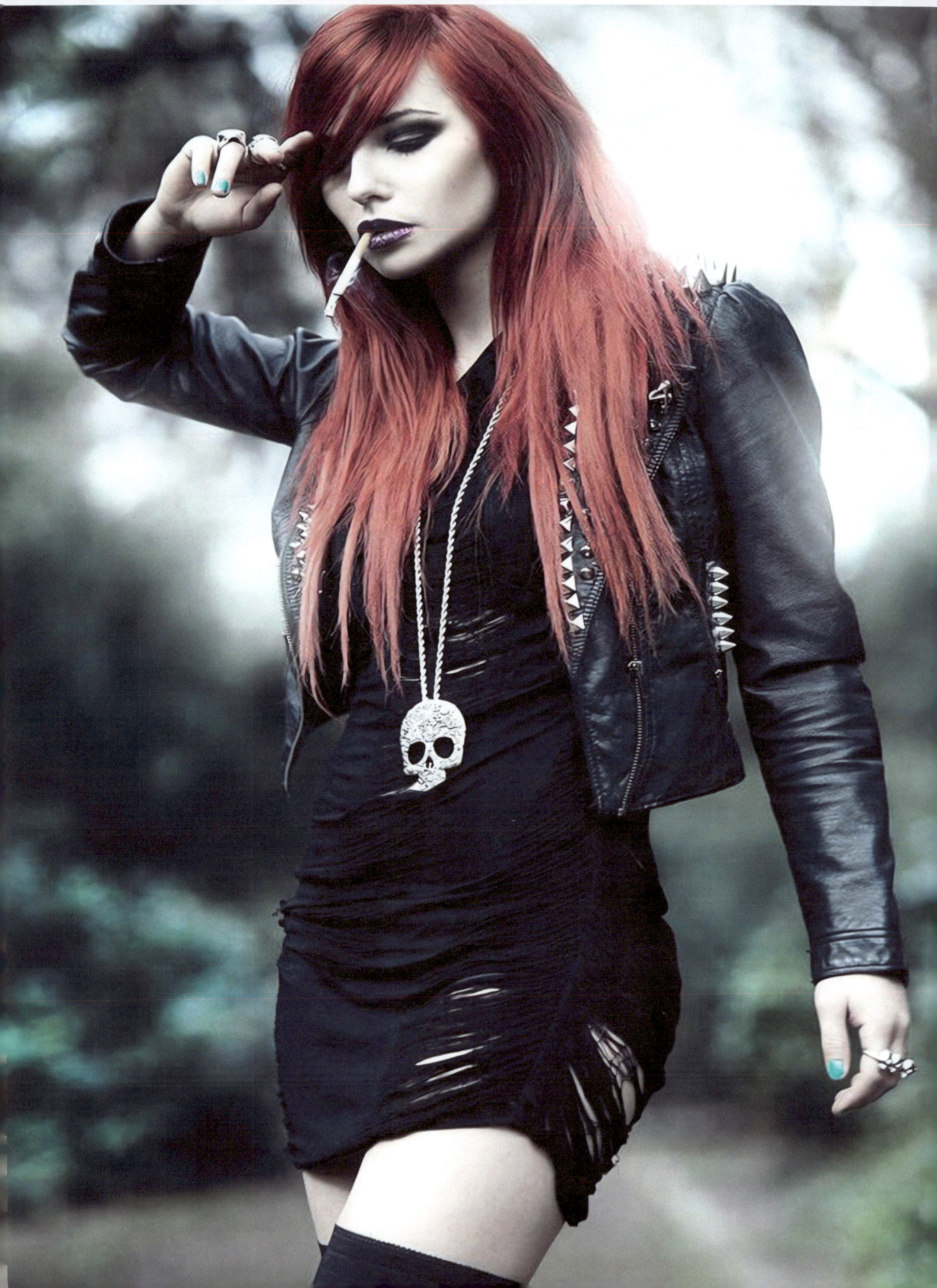

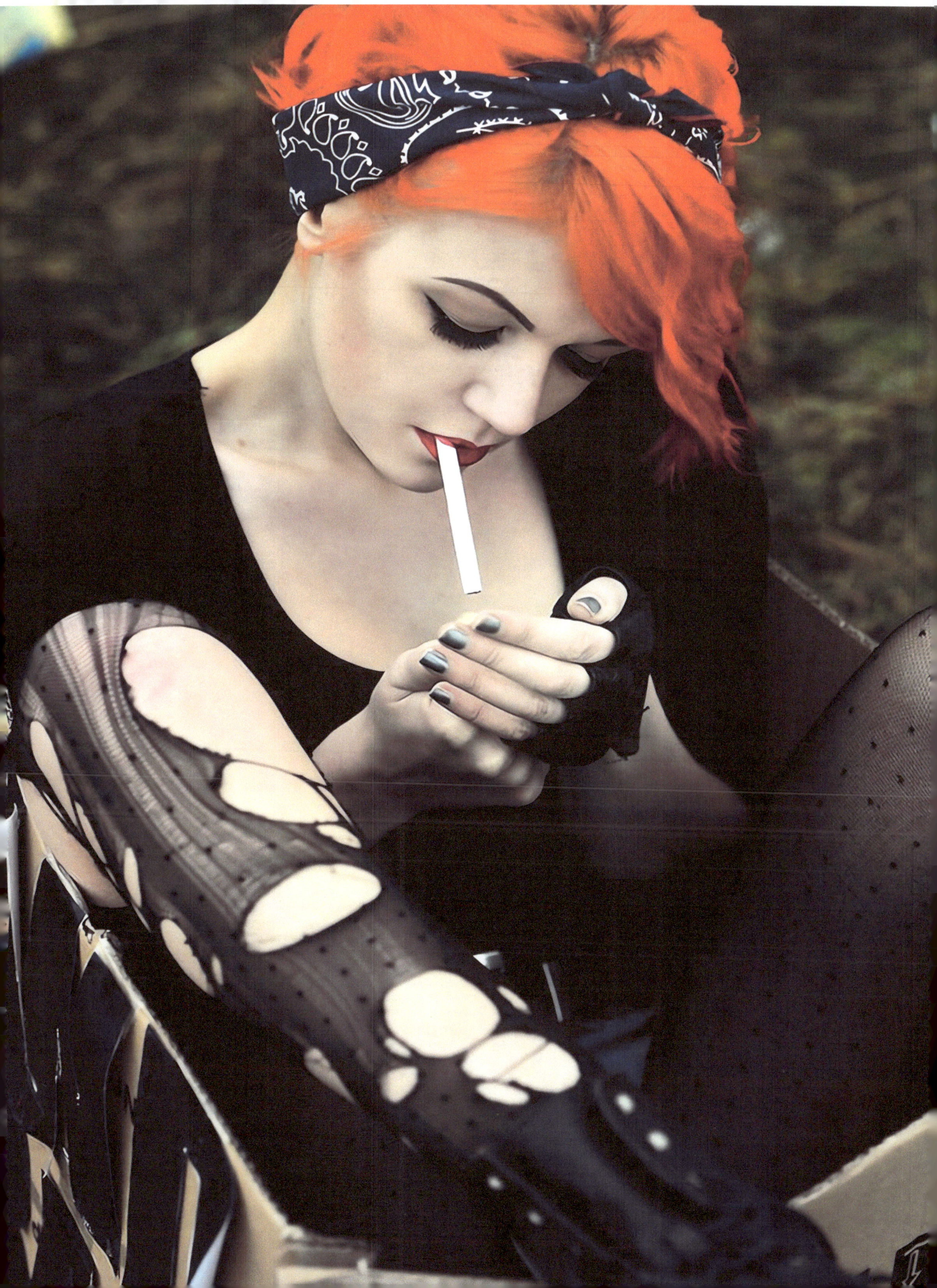

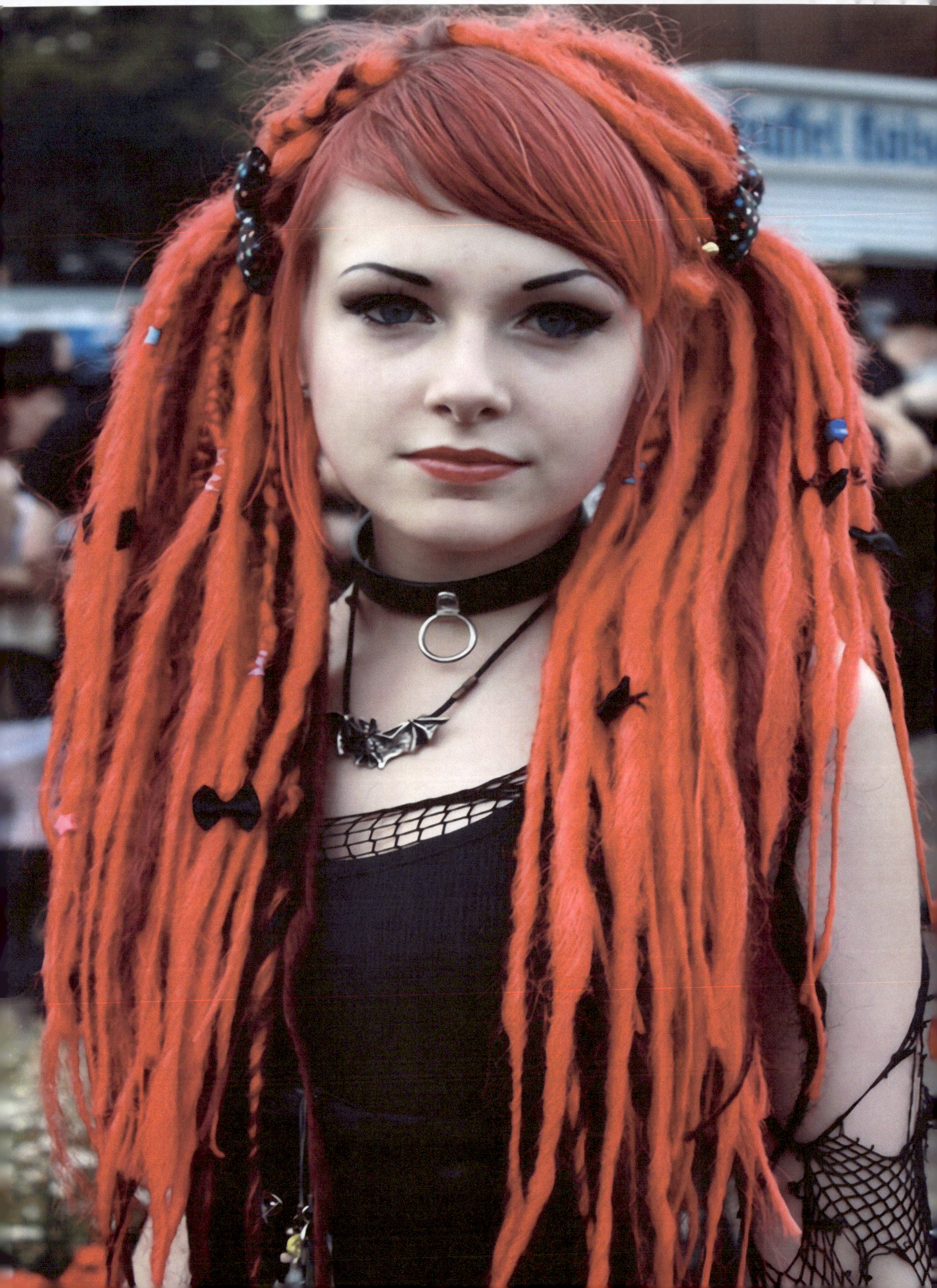

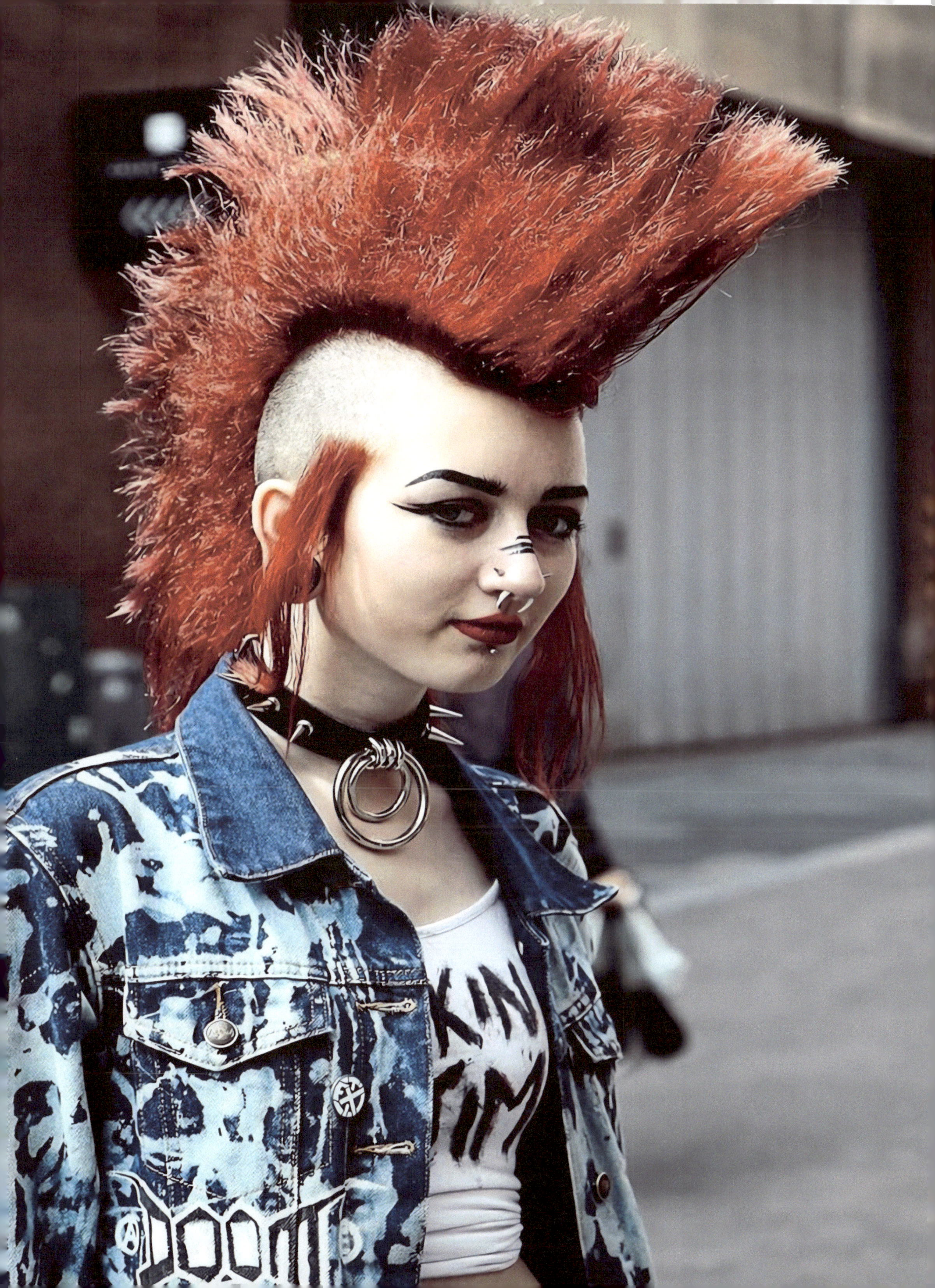

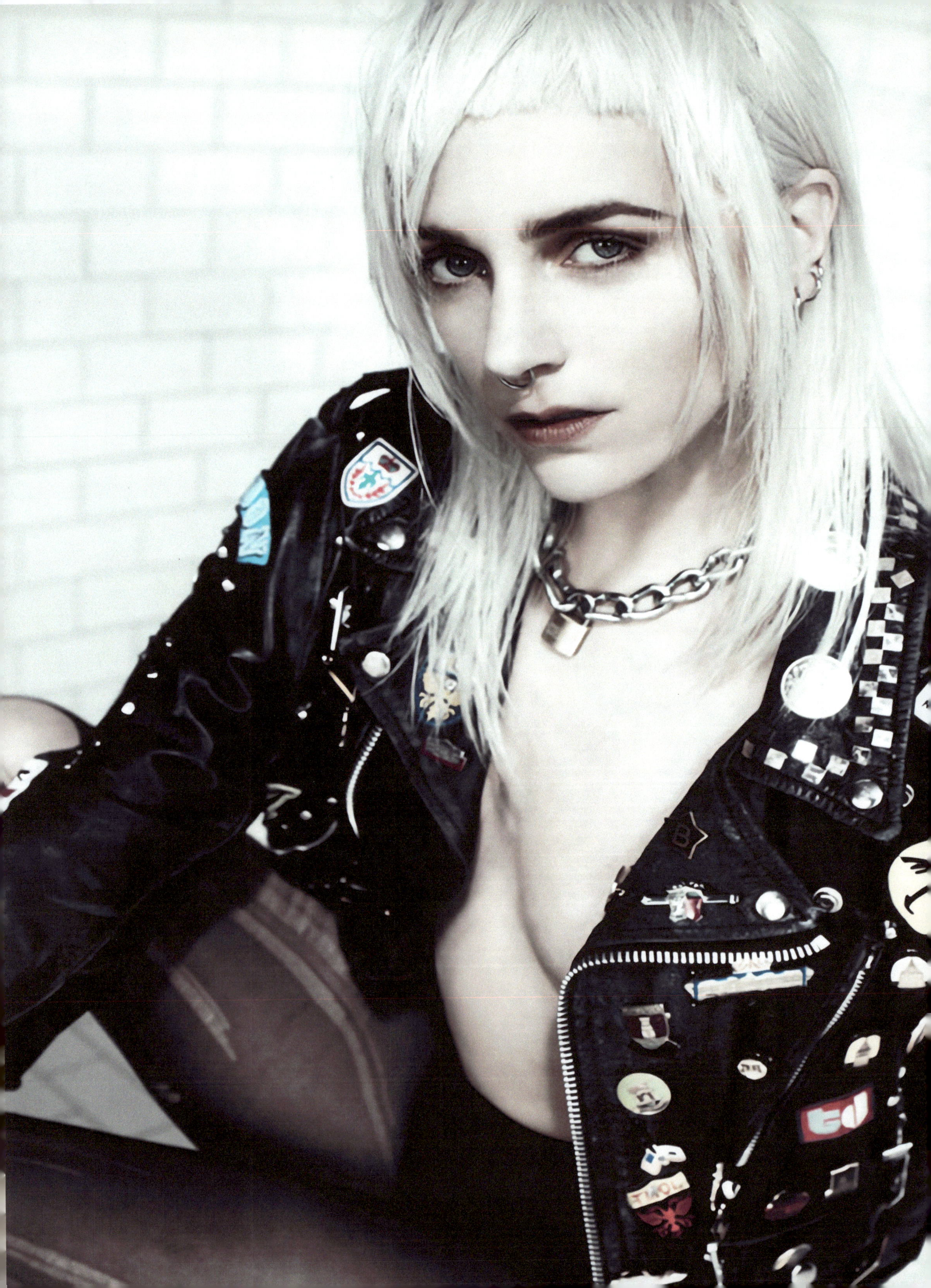